# Babies' Names

This is a Parragon Book
First published in 2001

Parragon
Queen Street House
4 Queen Street
Bath BA1 1HE, UK



ISBN: 0-75255-190-6



A copy of the CIP data for this book is available from the British Library upon request.



Editorial, design and layout by Essential Books, 7 Stucley Place, London NW1 8NS

Printed and bound in China

# Babies' Names

Noam Friedlander

# INTRODUCTION

Choosing a name for your child is probably one of the most important things you will ever do for him or her. A name can be a reflection of character and identity and is an important first impression by which people are judged. When you peruse this book to choose a name, bear in mind the following hints. Good luck!

Some parents like to choose names that have important or meaningful associations – whether they are places, emotions or family names. You might want to choose a name that reminds you of something significant. You can name your child after a family member, whether dead or alive, though remember that some religious cultures consider it bad luck to name a child after a living member of the family. To avoid this you could always change the name slightly or choose an alternative version of it.

There are no rules that say you have to pick a name from your own ethnic background. Celtic and Irish names have become more popular over the last few years, as well as names from African or Japanese cultures. However, some people think that taking a name from your own particular heritage can offer a source of identity to your child.

Some people worry about choosing names such as Frances

that do not clearly define their child's gender, while others consider it less important. Obviously, if you have a problem with ambiguous names then these should be the first names off your list.

Some parents go for unusual names to avoid the problem of their child having the same name as many others. It is hard to strike a balance and find a name that is distinctive and exclusive but isn't too unusual or odd. There are advantages and disadvantages to having an ordinary or a unique name. While the common names might be easier to spell or pronounce, an unusual name might make your child stand out and feel special. Just because some names cause difficulties due to people's unfamiliarity with them, it doesn't mean you should be put off choosing them.

Be careful to make sure your child's initials don't spell or represent anything undesirable, especially when you include the middle names. You don't want to give your child a name such as Charles Robert Andrew Peterson (CRAP) or Patsy Isabelle Grant (PIG).

For some people it is important to choose a name with an upbeat meaning, as this positive meaning will be associated with your child. You can chose names that refer to qualities or traits that you hope your child will have, names with meanings that might have special significance for you, or names that describe physical qualities that might already be obvious in your baby. For instance, Silas means 'snub-nosed' and Ciera means 'little dark one'.

Make sure your child's first name doesn't sound foolish when added to your surname. For example, someone with the last name Land should probably not be called Scott and someone with the last name Walker should possibly not be given the name Luke, especially with the middle name Sky! If you have an common surname, like Smith or Jones, an exciting or unusual name can spice it up a bit. For example, John Smith or Anne Jones could become Finbar Smith or Bronwyn Jones.

Before picking that special name, think about ways it can be shortened. Some nicknames may sound foolish alongside the child's surname. Some examples would be Sarah Pally (Sally Pally), Sylvester Fox (Sly Fox) or Stephen Grieve (Steve Grieve). Your child could insist on using their formal name, rather than the nickname, but this might not always be possible, especially if they're being teased at school or by their work colleagues.

You may want to pick a name that has lot of nicknames and variations, such as Elizabeth or John, so that your child will have more control over his or her name when they're older. The only danger in doing this is that a childhood nickname may stick through adult life and could sound foolish.

Some names never go out of the most popular names lists –

names like Jack and Thomas or Lucy and Emma. However, names do tend to follow trends or cycles of popularity and are often influenced by popular figures of the time. Back in the 1930s the name Shirley dominated top ten lists due to the popularity of Shirley Temple. Later there was Ryan, for Ryan O'Neal and even Demi, after Demi Moore, appeared in the top 100 list back in 1994. In the late 1990s names like Britney and Tiffany all made appearances in the top 100.

When choosing your child's name, try to be objective and sure that the name will sound just as good in fifty years or so. Your child may not appreciate being named after pop or TV icons from the 'ancient' past.

Before finalising your child's name, it is a good idea to chat to your friends and family to ask their opinion (though this can lead to family rows!). Not everyone will agree with your choice but they might provide some welcome help.

# Boys

## A

**Aaron**: From the Hebrew meaning 'lofty', 'inspired' or 'mountaineer'. Alternative spellings: Aaran, Aarao, Aharon, Aranne, Arek, Aren, Arin, Aron, Aronek, Aronne, Aronos, Haroun, Harun. Short forms: Ari, Arni, Ron, Ronnie, Ronny.

**Aban**: From the Irish Gaelic meaning 'a little abbot'. Alternative spelling: Abban.

**Abasi**: From the Swahili meaning 'stern'.

**Abdul**: From the Arabic *abd* meaning 'servant of'. Short form: Abdi.

**Abdullah**: From the Arabic meaning 'servant of Allah'. Alternative spellings: Abdalla, Abdulla. Short forms: Abdal, Abdul, Del.

**Abel**: From the Hebrew meaning 'vanity'or 'breath' or the Assyrian meaning 'son'. Short forms: Abe, Abie.

**Abelard**: From the Middle English meaning 'guardian of the abbey larder'.

**Abi**: From the Turkish meaning 'elder brother'.

**Abid**: From the Arabic meaning 'servant'.

**Abir**: From the Hebrew meaning 'strong', 'heroic'.

**Abishai**: From the Hebrew meaning 'my father's gift'. Alternative spelling: Abisha.

**Abishur**: From the Hebrew meaning 'my father's glance/look'.

**Abner**: From the Hebrew meaning 'the Father is light'. Alternative spelling: Ebner.

**Abraham**: From the Hebrew meaning 'father of many'. Alternative spellings: Abrahim, Abrahamo, Abrahan, Abram, Avraham, Avram, Avrum, Ibrahim. Short forms: Ab, Abe, Abi, Bram.

**Absalom**: From the Hebrew meaning 'Father is peace'. Alternative spelling: Absolom.

**Acar**: From the Turkish meaning 'bright'.

**Acayib**: From the Turkish meaning 'wonderful and strange'.

**Ace**: From the Latin *as* meaning 'unity'.

**Achilles**: From Greek mythology, the son of Peleus and the sea-nymph Thetis. Alternative spelling: Achille, Achilleus.

**Ackley**: From the Middle English *akern* meaning 'acorn' and *ley* meaning 'meadow' thus 'meadow of the oak trees'.

**Acton**: From the Old English *ac* meaning 'oak' and *tun* meaning 'village' thus 'village of oak trees'.

**Adair**: From the Scottish Gaelic *athdara* meaning 'from the oak-tree ford'; see also Edgar.

**Adal**: From the German *adal* meaning 'noble'.

**Adalric**: From the German *adal* meaning 'noble' and *richi* meaning 'ruler', 'power', thus 'noble ruler'.

**Adam**: From the Hebrew *adamah* meaning 'red earth' or 'from the earth'. Alternative spellings: Ad, Adamec, Adamek, Adamik, Adamka, Adamko, Adamo, Adamok, Adan, Adao, Adas, Addis, Addy, Ade, Adem, Adhamh, Adi, Adnon, Adok, Adomas, Adrien, Damek, Deddy, Keady, Keddie.

**Adan**: From the Nigerian meaning 'a large bat'.

**Adar**: From the Syrian meaning 'ruler' or 'prince' or the Hebrew meaning 'fire'.

**Addison**: From Old English meaning 'Adam's son'.

**Adel**: From the Teutonic meaning 'noble'.

**Adelar**: From the Teutonic meaning 'noble eagle'.

**Adelard**: From the Teutonic meaning 'nobly resolute'.

**Aden**: See Aidan.

**Adiel**: From the Hebrew meaning 'God is an ornament'.

**Adin**: From the Hebrew meaning 'pleasure given' or the Old Norse meaning 'delicate'.

**Adir**: From the Hebrew meaning 'majestic' or 'noble'.

**Adlai**: From the Aramaic form of the Hebrew Adaliah meaning 'God is just'.

**Adler**: From the German or Old English meaning 'eagle'.

**Adnan**: From the Arabic meaning 'to settle'.

**Adolph**: From the Old German meaning 'noble' or 'wolf'. Alternative spellings: Adolf, Adophus. Short forms: Dolph, Dolphus.

**Adon**: From the Hebrew meaning 'belonging to the Lord'.

**Adonis**: From the Phoenician meaning 'lord'.

**Adri**: From the Hindi meaning 'rock'.

**Adrian**: From the Latin meaning 'man from Adria' (the Adriatic Sea region). Alternative spellings: Adriano, Adrien, Adrik. Adrion, Adron, Hadrian.

**Adriel**: From the Hebrew meaning 'of God's flock' or 'God's majesty'. Alternative spellings: Adri, Adial. Short form: Ari.

**Aeneas**: From the Greek meaning 'praised'. Alternative spellings: Angus, Eneas, Enne.

**Agamemnon**: From the Greek meaning 'resolute'.

**Agni**: From the Hindi god of fire.

**Ahab**: From the Hebrew meaning 'father's brother'.

**Ahearn**: From the Gaelic meaning 'owner of horses'. Alternative spellings: Ahern, Aherne, Hearn, Hearne.

**Ahmed**: From the Arabic meaning 'much praised'. Alternative spellings: Ahmad, Amad, Amadi.

**Aidan**: From the Gaelic meaning 'fire' or 'little fiery one' or the Latin *adjuvare* meaning 'to help' via the Middle English *eyeden* and *aiden*. Alternative spellings: Aden, Edan, Eden.

**Aiken**: From the Old English meaning 'made of oak'.

**Ain**: From the Scottish meaning 'own', 'belonging to oneself'.

**Ainmire**: From the Irish Gaelic meaning 'great lord'.

**Ainsley**: From the Scottish meaning 'own place' or 'my field'.

Alternative spellings: Anslee, Ansley, Anslie, Ansy.

**Ajay**: From the Skanskrit meaning 'invincible' or the Punjabi meaning 'victorious'.

**Al**: Short form of names beginning Al-.

**Alan**: The origin of this name is disputed, possibly from the Gaelic meaning 'fair', 'handsome', 'bright'; the Welsh meaning 'harmony', 'peace' or the Irish meaning 'noble'. Alternative spellings: Alain, Allen, Alun.

**Alard**: From the shortened version of the Old German name Athal meaning 'noble' and *hardu* meaning 'hard', 'tough and resilient', 'noble'.

**Alaric**: From the Old German meaning 'ruler over all'. Alternative spellings: Alarick, Alarik. Short forms: Rich, Ricky.

**Alasdair**: The Gaelic form of the Greek name Alexander meaning 'defender of men'. Alternative spellings: Alastair, Aldair, Alistair, Alister, Allister. Short forms: Al, Alec, Ali, Alick, Ally.

**Alban**: From the Latin meaning 'man from Alba' or 'blonde', 'fair one' or from the English meaning 'white'. Alternative spellings: Alben, Albin, Albinus, Albyn, Alva, Elva.

**Albern**: From the German meaning 'noble', 'courageous'.

**Alberic**: From the German meaning 'powerful elf'. Alternative spellings: Alberich, Auberon, Aubrey, Oberon.

**Albert**: From the Old English or German meaning 'noble and bright'. Alternative spellings: Albrik, Alberto, Alberk, Adelbert,

Aliberto, Alvertos, Aubert, Bechtel, Elbert. Short forms: Al, Albie, Bert, Bertie, Berto, Berty.

**Albion**: From the Latin meaning 'white cliffs'.

**Alden**: From the Old English meaning 'old' or 'wise protector'.

**Aldo**: From the Old German or Italian meaning 'old and wise'.

**Aldous**: From the Germanic name Aldo meaning 'old'. Alternative spelling: Eldon.

**Aldrich**: From the Old English meaning an 'old and wise ruler'. Alternative spellings: Aldric, Aldridge, Audric, Eldredge, Eldridge, Elric. Short forms: Al, Rich, Richie, Ricky.

**Aldwin**: From the Old English meaning 'wise and reliable friend'. Alternative spelling: Eldwin.

**Alex**: See Alexander. Alternative spellings: Alec, Alek, Alic, Alis.

**Aled**: From the Welsh meaning 'from the name of the river'.

**Alexander**: From the Latin form of the Greek name Alexandros, from alexin meaning 'to defend' and aner meaning 'man or warrior' thus 'man's defender and protector'. Alternative spellings: Alecsandar, Alejandro, Alekos, Aleksandar, Aleksander, Aleksandr, Alessandro, Alexandar, Alexandor, Alexandr, Alexandre, Alexandros, Alexsander, Alexzander, Alisander, Alixander, Alixandre. Short forms: Al, Alec, Alek, Aleksi, Alex, Alexis, Alick, Ally, Lex, Lech, Lecks, Sandro, Sacha, Sander, Sanders, Sandey, Sandor, Sandro, Sandy, Sasha, Saunder, Sauners, Sender, Zander.

**Alexis**: Shortened form of Alexander.

**Alfred**: From the German and Old English meaning 'good counsellor' or 'elf counsellor'. Alternative spellings: Aelfric, Ailfrid, Alfeo, Alfredo, Alfric, Alfrick, Alfrid, Alfris, Alured, Avere, Avery, Elfrid. Short forms: Alf, Alfie, Fred, Freddie, Freddy.

**Alger**: From the Old English meaning 'clever and quick-witted warrior'. Alternative spellings: Aelgar, Algar, Elgar.

**Algernon**: From the French meaning 'with a moustache'.

**Ali**: From the Arabic meaning 'the god', 'the highest', 'the greatest'.

**Aloysius**: From the Old German meaning 'famous warrior'; possibly also a Latin form of Louis.

**Alonso**: See Alphonse. Alternative spelling: Elonzo.

**Alphonse**: From the German meaning 'noble' or 'eager'. Alternative spellings: Alfonso, Alonzo, Alphons, Alphonso, Alphonsus. Short forms: Fonz, Fonzie, Lon, Lonnie.

**Alroy**: From the Spanish meaning 'king' or the Gaelic meaning 'red-haired youth'.

**Alvin**: From the German meaning 'noble friend' or the Latin meaning 'white' or 'light skinned'.

**Alwyn**: From the Old English meaning 'strong and wise woman'.

**Amadeus**: From the Latin meaning 'loves God'.

**Ambrose**: From the Greek meaning 'immortal'. Alternative spellings: Ambroise, Ambrosi, Ambrosius, Ambrus.

**Amiel**: From the Hebrew meaning 'God of my people'.

**Amin**: From the Persian meaning 'honest', 'trustworthy'.

**Amir**: From the Arabic meaning 'prince'.

**Amon**: From the Hebrew meaning 'faithful'.

**Amos**: From the Hebrew meaning 'burdened', 'troubled'.

**Anastasius**: From the Greek meaning 'resurrection'.

**Anatole**: From the Greek meaning 'east' or 'raising sun'.

**Anders**: From the Scandinavian or the Greek meaning 'manliness' or 'virility'.

**Andreas**: See Andrew. Short form: Andre.

**Andrew**: From the Greek meaning 'manly'. Alternative spellings: Adre, Andor, Andre, Andra, Andras, Andreas, Andrei, Andres, Anker, Druhan. Short forms: Andy, Drew.

**Angel**: From the Greek meaning 'angel' or the Latin meaning 'messenger'. Alternative spellings: Angelo, Angelito.

**Angus**: From the Celtic meaning 'unique choice' derived from the Gaelic name Aonghus. Alternative spellings: Aonghus, Ennis. Short form: Gus.

**Anil**: From the Hindi meaning 'wind god'.

**Annas**: From the Greek meaning 'gift from God'. Alternative spellings: Anis, Anna, Annais.

**Ansel**: From the French meaning 'follower of a nobleman'.

**Anselm**: From the German meaning 'divine protector' or 'helmet of God'.

**Anthony**: From the Latin meaning 'praiseworthy' or 'priceless' or the Greek meaning 'flourishing'. Alternative spellings: Anthonu, Antjuan, Antoine, Antonio, Antony, Antwan. Short forms: Antal, Anton, Toni, Tony.

**Antoine:** See Anthony.

**Antti**: From the Finnish meaning 'manly'.

**Anwar**: From the Arabic meaning 'luminous'.

**Apollo**: From the Greek meaning 'manly', 'to reply' or 'to destroy'.

**Aquilla**: From the Latin and Spanish meaning 'eagle'.

**Archibald**: From the German meaning 'bold'. Alternative spellings: Archaimbaud, Archibaldo, Arkady. Short forms: Arch, Archi.

**Ardal**: From the Gaelic meaning 'highly courageous' or the Irish version of Arnold.

**Arden**: From the Latin meaning 'ardent', 'fiery'.

**Argus**: From the Greek meaning 'bright-eyed' or 'highly observant'.

**Ari**: A shortened form of Ariel, Arion or Aristotle.

**Ariel**: From the Hebrew meaning 'lion of god'. Alternative spellings: Ariell, Ariya, Ariyel, Arrial, Arriel. Short forms: Ari, Arel, Areli.

**Aries**: From the Latin meaning 'ram'.

**Arif**: From the Arabic meaning 'knowledgeable'.

**Arion**: From the Greek meaning 'enchanted' or the Hebrew meaning 'melodious'. Alternative spellings: Arian, Ariane,

Arien. Short form: Ari.

**Aristotle:** From the Greek meaning 'best'. Short form: Ari.

**Arlo:** From the Spanish meaning 'barberry' or the English meaning 'fortified hill'.

**Armand:** From the Latin meaning 'noble' or the German meaning 'soldier'. Alternative spellings: Armad, Armando, Armands, Armani, Armon, Armondo.

**Arno:** From the German meaning 'eagle wolf'.

**Arnold:** From the old German meaning 'strength' or 'eagle'. Alternative spellings: Ardal, Arnaud, Arnault, Arnoll. Short forms: Arne, Arnie.

**Arne:** From the Scandinavian meaning 'eagle', see also Arnold.

**Arran:** From the Scottish taken from the place name or meaning 'island dweller'.

**Arsenio:** From the Greek meaning 'masculine'.

**Artemus:** From the Greek meaning 'gift of Artemis'. Alternative spellings: Artemio, Artemis, Artimis, Artimus.

**Arthur:** The origin of this name is disputed. It is either from the Irish meaning 'noble' or 'lofty hill'; the Celtic meaning 'bear'; the Old English meaning 'rock' or the Icelandic meaning 'follower of Thor'. Alternative spellings: Artek, Arther, Arthor, Artor, Arturo, Arturus, Artus, Aurthur. Short forms: Art, Arte, Arti, Artie, Arto, Arty, Artur.

**Arvel:** From the Welsh meaning 'wept over'.

**Arvid:** From the Hebrew meaning 'wanderer' or the Scandinavian meaning 'man of the people'. Alternative spellings: Arvad, Arvind. Short forms: Arv, Arve, Arvie.

**Asa:** From the Hebrew meaning 'physician', 'healer'.

**Asad:** From the Arabic meaning 'lion'.

**Ash:** From the Old English meaning 'ash tree'; see also Ashley.

**Asher:** From the Hebrew meaning 'what happiness' or 'blessed'.

**Ashley:** From the Old English meaning 'ash tree meadow'. Alternative spellings: Ashliegh, Ashli, Ashlie, Ashly, Ashlyn, Ashlynn.

**Ashton:** From the Old English *æsc* meaning 'ash' and *tun* 'enclosure or settlement'

**Aswad:** From the Arabic meaning 'dark skinned', 'black'.

**Athol:** From the Old English meaning 'noble'.

**Atlas:** From the Greek meaning 'lifted', 'carried'.

**Atley:** From the Old English meaning 'meadow'.

**Attila:** From the Gothic meaning 'little father'.

**Auberon:** From the German meaning 'noble' or 'bearlike'. Alternative spellings: Aubrey, Avery, Oberon.

**Aubrey:** From the German meaning 'noble'; the French meaning 'blond ruler' or possibly from *alb* meaning 'elf' and *ric* meaning 'power'. Alternative spellings: Aubree, Aubrie, Aubury.

**Auden:** From the English meaning 'old friend'.

**Audric:** From the English meaning 'wise ruler'.

**Augustine**: From the Latin meaning 'majestic'. Alternative spellings: Agostino, Aguistin, Agustin, Augustus, Austin. Short forms: August, Augie.

**Aurek**: From the Polish meaning 'golden-haired'.

**Aurelius**: From the Latin meaning 'golden'. Short form: Aurelio.

**Austin**: From the Latin meaning 'the venerable one'; see also Augustine. Alternative spelling: Austen.

**Avi**: From the Hebrew meaning 'God is my father'.

**Aviv**: From the Hebrew meaning 'youth' or 'springtime'.

**Axel**: From the Latin meaning 'axe'; the German meaning 'small oak tree' or the Scandinavian meaning 'source of life' or 'divine reward'.

**Aylmer**: From the Old English meaning 'noble and famous'. Alternative spelling: Aymer, Elmer.

## B

**Bahir**: From the Arabic meaning 'brilliant', 'dazzling'.

**Bailey**: From the French meaning 'bailiff', 'steward' or the Middle English meaning 'outer wall of a castle'. Alternative spellings: Bailie, Baillie, Baily, Bayley, Bayly.

**Baldrick**: From the German meaning 'brave ruler' or 'bold ruler'. Alternative spellings: Baldric, Baudric.

**Baldwin**: From the German meaning 'bold friend'. Alternative spellings: Balduin, Baudoin, Baldwyn.

**Balfour**: From the Celtic meaning 'pasture land' or the Old English meaning 'distant hill'.

**Balthasar**: From the Greek meaning 'may God protect the king'. Alternative spellings: Baltasar, Balthazar, Belshazzar.

**Balu**: From the Sanskrit meaning 'young'.

**Barclay**: From the Celtic and Old English meaning 'birch tree meadow'. Alternative spellings: Barcley, Berkeley.

**Barnabas**: From the Hebrew meaning 'son of exhortation'. Alternative spellings: Barnaby, Barnebus. Short forms: Barna, Barney, Barnie.

**Barney**: From the Greek or Hebrew meaning 'son of prophecy' or 'consolation'; see also Barnabus.

**Barnum**: From the German meaning 'barn', 'storage place' or the English meaning 'baron's home'.

**Baron**: From the Middle Latin meaning 'man' or 'warrior'.

**Barry**: From the Old Celtic name Bearrach meaning 'spear' or 'good marksman'; the Gaelic Irish name Fionnbharr meaning 'white haired' or the the Welsh meaning 'son of Harry'. Alternative spellings: Barri, Barrie.

**Bartholomew**: From the Aramaic meaning 'son of Talmai'. Short forms: Bart, Bartie.

**Barton**: From the English *bere* meaning 'barley' and *tun* meaning 'enclosure' thus 'barley farm'.

**Bartram**: From the Scandinavian meaning 'glorious raven'.

**Baruch**: From the Hebrew meaning 'blessed'.

**Basil**: From the Greek *basileios* meaning 'kingly' or the Irish Gaelic meaning 'war of strife'. Alternative spellings: Basel, Basile, Bazil, Basilio, Basle, Vassily. Short forms: Bas, Baz.

**Basil**: From the Greek *basileios* meaning 'kingly' or the Irish Gaelic meaning 'war of strife'. Alternative spellings: Basel, Basile, Bazil, Basilio, Vassily. Short forms: Bas, Baz.

**Bassett**: From the English meaning 'little person'.

**Beau**: From the French meaning 'handsome', 'beautiful'. Alternative spelling: Bo.

**Beaufort**: From the French meaning 'beautiful fort'.

**Beaumont**: From the French meaning 'beautiful mountain'.

**Beauregard**: From the French meaning 'handsome', 'beautiful', 'well-regarded'.

**Beck**: From the Old Norse meaning 'brook'.

**Bede**: From the Middle English meaning 'prayer'.

**Bela**: From the Czech meaning 'white' or the Hungarian meaning 'bright'.

**Belvedere**: From the Italian meaning 'beautiful to look at' or 'a vantage point for a fine view'. Alternative spelling: Belveder.

**Bellamy**: From the French meaning 'beautiful friend'.

**Ben**: From the Hebrew meaning 'son' or the Scottish Gaelic meaning 'peak'; see also Benedict and Benjamin.

**Benedict**: From the Latin meaning 'blessed'. Alternative spellings:

Bendick, Bendict, Benedik, Bendix, Benedetto, Benedicto, Benedictus, Benito, Benoit. Short forms: Ben, Beni.

**Benjamin**: From the Hebrew meaning 'son of my right hand'. Alternative spellings: Bejamin, Beniam, Bengamon, Benjaman, Mincho. Short forms: Benjy, Benny, Ben.

**Bennett**: From the Latin meaning 'little one'. Alternative spelling: Benoit.

**Beno**: From the Hebrew meaning 'son'.

**Bentley**: From the Old English meaning 'moor', 'course grass meadow'.

**Ben-Zion**: From the Hebrew meaning 'son of Zion'.

**Beppe**: See Joseph.

**Beren**: Based on a name from Tolkien's *Lord of the Rings* meaning 'bearlike' or a shortened version of the Teutonic name Berenger.

**Bernard**: From the German meaning 'brave as a bear'. Alternative spellings: Barnardo, Bearnard, Bernadas, Bernardin, Bernardo, Barnardus, Bernek, Bernhard, Bjorn, Burnard, Bernd. Short forms: Bern, Bernie, Berno.

**Bert**: From the German meaning 'bright'; also a short form of Albert and Berthold.

**Berthold**: From the Old High German meaning 'bright', 'illustrious' or 'brilliant ruler'. Alternative spellings: Bertold, Bertolde, Bertus. Short forms: Bert, Bertie, Burt.

**Bertram**: From the Old German meaning 'bright' or

'illustrious/bright raven'.

**Bertrand:** From the German meaning 'bright shield'.

**Berwyn:** From the English meaning 'harvest son'.

**Bevan:** From the Welsh meaning 'son of Evan'.

**Beverly:** From the English meaning 'beaver meadow'. Alternative spellings: Beverlea, Beverley.

**Bevis:** From the French meaning 'bull'.

**Bill:** See William.

**Birgir:** From the Norwegian meaning 'rescued'.

**Blaine:** From the Irish meaning 'thin', 'lean' or the English meaning 'river source'. Alternative spellings: Blane, Blayne.

**Blair:** From the Celtic meaning 'place' or the Irish meaning 'plain/field'.

**Blake:** From the Old English meaning 'dark meadow' or the Old Norse meaning 'shining', 'white'.

**Blaze:** From the Latin meaning 'stammerer' or the English meaning 'flame/trail mark made on a tree'. Alternative spelling: Blaise.

**Blythe:** From the English meaning 'carefree'.

**Boaz:** From the Hebrew meaning 'swift' or 'strong'. Alternative spellings: Bo, Bos, Boz.

**Bob:** See Robert.

**Boden:** From the Scandinavian meaning 'sheltered' or the French meaning 'messenger' or 'herald'.

**Borak:** From the Arabic or Hebrew meaning 'lightning'. Alternative spelling: Borak.

**Borg:** From the Scandinavian meaning 'castle'.

**Boris:** From the Slavic meaning 'battler', 'warrior' or the Russian meaning 'fight'.

**Bourne:** From the Latin or French meaning 'boundary' or the English meaning 'brook', 'stream'.

**Boyd:** From the Celtic meaning 'yellow-haired'.

**Bradley:** From the Old English meaning 'broad meadow'. Short form: Brad.

**Brady:** From the Irish meaning 'spirited' or the English meaning 'broad island'.

**Bram:** From the Celtic meaning 'bramble', 'brushwood'; also a diminutive form of Abraham.

**Bramwell:** From the English meaning 'bramble-bush spring'.

**Brandeis:** From the Czech meaning 'dweller on a burned clearing'.

**Brandon:** From the Old English *brom* and *dun* meaning 'gorse hill' or 'beacon hill'. Alternative spellings: Brandan, Brandin, Brannon. Short forms: Bran, Brand.

**Brede:** From the Scandinavian meaning 'iceberg', 'glacier'.

**Brendan:** From the Irish meaning 'little raven' or the Gaelic meaning 'prince'. Alternative spellings: Brennan, Brenndan, Bryn.

**Brent:** From the Old English meaning 'steep hill'. Alternative spelling: Brenton.

**Brett**: From the Gaelic meaning 'Great Britain' or the Old French meaning 'a person from Brittany'. Alternative spellings: Brit, Brittain, Brittan, Britten.

**Brian**: From the Irish Gaelic meaning 'strong', 'virtuous' or 'honourable' or the Greek meaning 'strong'. Alternative spellings: Brano, Briant, Brion, Bryon, Bryan, Brin, Briny, Bryant.

**Brice**: From the Welsh meaning 'alert' or 'ambitious'; the English meaning 'son of Rice' or 'son of the ardent one' or the Celtic meaning 'strong' or 'brave'. Alternative spelling: Bryce.

**Brock**: From the Old English broc meaning 'badger'.

**Broderick**: From the Welsh meaning 'son of the famous ruler'; the English meaning 'broad ridge' or the Celtic meaning 'brother'. Alternative spellings: Broderic, Brodric, Brodrick. Short forms: Brod, Broddie.

**Brodie**: From the Irish meaning 'ditch/canal builder'; also a pet form of the Scandinavian name Broder meaning 'brother'. Alternative spellings: Brodi, Brody.

**Bronson**: From the English meaning 'son of Brown'.

**Brook**: From the English meaning 'brook', 'stream'.

**Brooklyn**: From the area of New York City.

**Brosnan**: From the Irish Gaelic meaning 'one from Brosna' in Ireland or 'dweller near the Brosna river'.

**Bruce**: From the Old French meaning 'brushwood thicket', 'woods'.

**Bruno:** From Old German *brun* meaning 'brown'.

**Brutus:** From the Latin meaning 'heavy', 'irrational', 'stupid' or 'unreasonable'.

**Bryan:** See Brian.

**Bryce:** See Brice.

**Bryson:** From the Welsh *brych* meaning 'speckled'. Alternative spelling: Bricen.

**Bryn:** From the Welsh meaning 'hill or mound'.

**Brynmor:** From the Welsh meaning 'great hill'.

**Bud:** From the English meaning 'herald', 'messenger'.

**Burt:** See Albert or Burton.

**Burton:** From the English meaning 'fortified town'. Short form: Burt.

**Busby:** From the Celtic meaning 'village in the thicket'.

**Byron:** From the French meaning 'cottage' or the Old English meaning 'barn'.

## C

**Cade:** From the Old French *catanus*, the name of a juniper tree.

**Cadell:** From the Welsh meaning 'battle'.

**Caden:** From the Irish meaning 'spirit of battle'.

**Cadfael:** From the Welsh meaning 'battle metal'.

**Cadmus:** From the Greek meaning 'from the east'.

**Cadogan:** From the Old Welsh meaning 'battle glory'.

**Cahan:** See Kane.

**Cahil**: From the Turkish meaning 'young native'.

**Cain**: See Kane.

**Cairn**: From the Welsh meaning 'landmark piled up with stones'.

**Caius**: From the Latin meaning 'rejoice'.

**Caldwell**: From the English meaning 'cold well'.

**Caleb**: Possibly from the Hebrew meaning 'dog'. Short form: Cale.

**Calhoun**: From the Irish meaning 'narrow woods' or the Scottish meaning 'warrior'.

**Callum**: From the Latin, French or Scottish Gaelic meaning 'dove', derived from the Latin name Columba. Alternative spelling: Calum.

**Calvin**: From the French or Latin meaning 'little bald one'.

**Cameron**: From the Gaelic meaning 'crooked nose'.

**Campbell**: From the Celtic meaning 'curved' or 'crooked mouth' or the Latin meaning 'beautiful field'.

**Canute**: From the Latin meaning 'white-haired' or the Scandinavian meaning 'knot'.

**Caradoc**: From the Celtic meaning 'love', 'beloved'.

**Carl**: See Charles. Alternative spellings: Karl, Carlos.

**Carlton**: From the Old English meaning 'settlement of the [free] peasants'.

**Carmichael**: From the Scottish meaning 'follower of Michael'.

**Carmine**: From the Latin meaning 'song' or 'crimson'.

**Carney**: From the Irish meaning 'victorious' or the Scottish meaning 'fighter'. Short form: Car.

**Carson**: Possibly from the English meaning 'son of Car'.

**Carter**: From the English meaning 'cart driver'.

**Carwyn**: From the Welsh meaning 'blessed love'.

**Cary**: From the Greek meaning 'pure' or the Welsh meaning 'castle' or 'rocky island'. Alternative spelling: Carey.

**Casey**: From the Celtic meaning 'brave in battle'.

**Casimir**: From the Slavic meaning 'peace-maker'. Alternative spellings: Casimer, Kazimir, Kazmer. Short form: Cass.

**Caspar**: From the German meaning 'imperial'. Alternative spellings: Casper, Gaspar, Jaspar, Kaspa, Kaspar, Kasper.

**Caspian**: Created by C S Lewis in his books on Narnia, but could be derived from the Persian *caspa* meaning 'treasurer'.

**Cassidy**: Possibly from the Welsh meaning 'trickster' or the Irish meaning 'curly-haired' or 'clever'.

**Cassius**: From the Latin meaning 'box' or 'protective cover'.

**Castor**: From the Greek meaning 'beaver'.

**Cathal**: From the Irish Gaelic meaning 'battle mighty'.

**Cecil**: From the Latin meaning 'blind'.

**Cedric**: From the Celtic meaning 'model of generosity'. Alternative spelling: Cerdic. Short forms: Cad, Rick, Ricky.

**Cemlyn**: From the Welsh meaning 'bent lake'.

**Ceri**: From the Welsh meaning 'love'.

**Chad**: Possibly from the English meaning 'warrior'.

**Chadwick**: From the Old English meaning 'dairy farm' or 'warrior's farm'.

**Chaim**: From the Hebrew meaning 'life'.

**Chance**: From the Old English meaning 'good fortune'.

**Chancellor**: From the Old English meaning 'secretary to the throne'.

**Chandler**: From the Old French meaning 'candle maker'.

**Charles**: From the Old German meaning 'free man'. Alternative spellings: Karl, Carl, Carlos. Short forms: Charlie.

**Chester**: From the Latin legionary camp of that name.

**Chet**: From the Thai meaning 'brother'.

**Chevy**: From the French *chevalier* meaning 'horseman' or 'knight'.

**Chris**: See Christopher or Christian.

**Christian**: From the Latin meaning the 'follower of Christ'. Alternative spelling: Christiano, Christianos, Christien, Chrystian, Crysek, Christiao, Christiano, Cristian, Krist, Krista, Kristian, Kristos, Krysek, Krystian. Short forms: Chris, Christy, Christie, Chrys, Kris, Kristie, Kristy, Krys.

**Christie**: See Christopher or Christian.

**Christopher**: From the Greek *christoforus* meaning 'the bearer of Christ'. Alternate spelling: Cristobad, Christoforus, Christofer, Christoffer, Christophe, Kristofer, Kristoffer, Kristopher. Short forms: Chris, Christie, Cris, Cristo, Cristof, Kit, Kris, Kriss.

**Cian**: From the Irish Gaelic meaning 'ancient'.

**Ciaran**: From the Irish Gaelic meaning 'black'. Alternative spellings: Ciaron, Kieran, Kieron.

**Cid**: From the Spanish meaning 'lord'. Alternative spellings: Sid, Cyd.

**Cillian**: From the Irish Gaelic meaning 'strife', 'monastery' or 'church'.

**Clancy**: From the Irish Gaelic meaning 'red warrior'.

**Clarence**: From the English meaning 'a person from Clare' (the Suffolk town) or possibly from the Latin meaning 'clear' or 'victorious'.

**Clark**: From the Old English meaning 'learned man'. Alternative spelling: Clarke.

**Claude**: From the Latin meaning 'lame'. Alternative spellings: Claud, Claudius.

**Clayton**: From the Old English meaning 'clay enclosure' or 'settlement in the clay'. Short form: Clay.

**Clement**: From the Latin meaning 'mild' or 'merciful'. Alternative spellings: Clem, Clemence, Clemente, Clemento, Klement. Short forms: Clem, Clemmie.

**Clifford**: From the Old English meaning 'ford by the slope'. Short form: Cliff.

**Clifton**: From the Old English meaning 'settlement on the slope'.

**Clinton**: From the Middle English meaning 'hilltop town'. Short form: Clint.

**Clive**: From the Old English meaning 'steep/high rock face'.

**Clyde**: From the Welsh meaning 'heard from far away' or 'warm'.

**Cody**: From the Irish surname O Cuidighthigh meaning 'helpful person'. Alternative spellings: Codi, Codie, Kodi, Kody.

**Colbert**: From the Old French meaning 'bright' or 'famous'.

**Colby**: Possibly from the Old English meaning 'dark', 'dark-haired'; the Old German *colfor* for which there is no definite meaning, and *berht* meaning 'famous' or the Gaelic *colla* meaning 'high'.

**Cole**: From the Old English meaning 'charcoal' or the Latin meaning 'cabbage farmer'.

**Coleman**: From the Anglo Saxon meaning 'follower of the doves'; the Middle English meaning 'coal miner' or the Latin meaning 'cabbage farmer'.

**Colin**: From the Gaelic meaning 'youth'; see also Nicholas.

**Coll**: From the Old Celtic meaning 'high'.

**Colm**: From the Irish meaning 'dove'.

**Conall**: From the Old Celtic meaning 'strong wolf' or the Celtic meaning 'high and mighty'. Alternative spelling: Conal.

**Conan**: From the Gaelic meaning 'wolf'; the Celtic meaning 'high' or 'wisdom' or the Old Irish meaning 'lover of hounds'.

**Conlan**: From the Welsh meaning 'hero'.

**Conley**: From the Gaelic meaning 'pure'.

**Conn**: From the Irish Gaelic meaning 'chief'.

**Connor**: From the Gaelic name Conchobhar meaning 'high desire' or the Celtic meaning 'wise'.

**Conrad**: From the German meaning 'bold in counsel'; see also Curtis. Alternative spellings: Conrade, Conrado, Konrad. Short forms: Con, Connie, Conny, Cort, Curt, Kurt.

**Constant**: From the Latin meaning 'remain steadfast in faith'. Alternative spelling: Constantine.

**Corbin**: From the Anglo-Norman meaning 'crow'. Alternative spelling: Corbinian.

**Corey**: Possibly from the Irish meaning 'good peace' or 'hollow'. Alternative spelling: Cory.

**Corin**: From the Roman god Quirinus.

**Cormac**: From the Irish Gaelic meaning 'charioteer'; the Greek meaning 'tree trunk' or the Irish meaning 'raven's son'.

**Cornelius**: From the Latin meaning 'horn'. Short form: Cornell.

**Cooper**: From English meaning 'a man who makes barrels'.

**Cosmo**: From the Greek meaning 'order' or 'beauty'.

**Courtney**: From the French meaning 'short nose' or 'domain of Curtius'.

**Craig**: From the Celtic meaning 'rock'.

**Crawford**: From the Scottish meaning 'ford where crows gather'.

**Creighton**: From the Old English meaning 'settlement boundary'. Alternative spelling: Crichton.

**Crispin**: From the Latin meaning 'curly-haired'.

**Cromwell**: From the Welsh meaning 'winding stream'.

**Curtis:** From the Old French meaning 'courteous'. Alternative spelling: Conrad. Short forms: Curt, Kurt.

**Cuthbert:** From the Old English meaning 'known', 'famous' or 'bright'.

**Cynan:** From the Welsh meaning 'chief', 'outstanding'.

**Cyprian:** From the Latin meaning 'native of Cyprus'.

**Cyrano:** From Ancient Greek meaning 'of Cyrene'.

**Cyril:** From the Classic Greek meaning 'lord' or 'master'.

**Cyrus:** From the Greek meaning 'Lord' or the Persian meaning 'sun' or 'throne'.

## D

**Dacey:** From the Gaelic meaning 'southerner'.

**Dafydd:** A Welsh form of David.

**Dagan:** From the Hebrew meaning 'corn' or 'grain' or the Babylonian meaning 'little fish'.

**Dagwood:** From the English meaning 'shining forest'.

**Dai:** A Welsh form of David.

**Dakota:** From the Sioux meaning 'a friend'.

**Dale:** From the Old Norse meaning 'broad valley', 'hollow'.

**Dallas:** From the Scottish Gaelic meaning 'from the waterfall field'.

**Dalton:** From the Old English meaning 'from the hamlet in the valley'.

**Dalziel:** From the Scottish meaning 'small field'.

**Damian:** From the Greek meaning 'to tame/kill' or 'tamer of men'.

**Damon:** From the Greek meaning 'divine power', 'fate' or the Old English *doeg* meaning 'day'.

**Dan:** From the Hebrew meaning 'judge'; see also Daniel.

**Dane:** From the Old Norse meaning 'Danish'; see also Daniel.

**Daniel:** From the Hebrew meaning 'God has judged', 'God is my judge'. Alternative spellings: Daneil, Danek, Daniela, Danil, Danya. Short forms: Dan, Dana, Dane, Danek, Danko, Dano, Dannie, Danny, Donal.

**Dante:** From the Italian meaning 'to endure', 'to last'.

**Darby:** From the Old Norse meaning 'one from the deer estate' or the Irish Gaelic meaning 'a free man'. Alternative spellings: Derby, Diarmaid.

**Darcy:** From the Irish Gaelic meaning 'a dark man'.

**Darian:** A contemporary form of Darius.

**Darius:** From the Greek meaning 'prosperous' or 'rich' or the Latin *daraya* meaning 'to possess'. Alternative spelling: Darrius. Short forms: Dario, Deny.

**Darnell:** From the Old English meaning 'from the hidden/secret nook'.

**Darrel:** From the Old English meaning 'darling', 'dear', 'beloved', 'special'. Alternative spellings: Darel, Darrell, Darryl, Derril.

**Darren:** From the Irish meaning 'dearly beloved' or 'small and great' or the Greek meaning 'wealthy'. Alternative spellings: Darien, Darin, Dario, Daron, Darran, Darrin, Darron, Darun, Daryn.

**Darrick**: See Derek.

**Darrow**: From the Old English meaning 'spear'.

**Darshan**: From the Sanskrit meaning 'to see'.

**Darwin**: From the Old English meaning 'lover of the sea' or 'beloved friend'.

**Darryl**: See Darrel.

**David**: From the Hebrew meaning 'beloved'. Alternative spellings: Dafyd, Dafydd, Dai, Davide, Davin, Davis, Dawe, Dawes, Dawson, Devi, Dewi, Dov, Dow. Short forms: Dave, Davi, Davey, Davy, Tab, Taffy.

**Dax**: From the town in Western France.

**Deacon**: From the Greek meaning 'servant'.

**Dean**: Possibly from the Old English meaning 'valley' or the Latin meaning 'leader of ten'. Short form: Dino.

**Decimus**: From the Latin meaning 'tenth'.

**Declan**: Possibly from the Irish meaning 'son of prayer'.

**Deepak**: From the Sanskrit meaning 'little lamp' or 'shining'; also the Hindu god of love.

**Deinol**: From the Welsh meaning 'attractive', 'charming'. Alternative spelling: Deiniol.

**Delano**: From the Irish Gaelic meaning 'healthy, dark man' or the Old French meaning 'from the nut tree place'.

**Delany**: From the Irish Gaelic meaning 'the challenger's descendent'.

**Delbert**: From the Old English meaning 'bright day', 'sunny day'.

**Delmar:** From the Latin meaning 'from the sea'. Alternative spelling: Delmar.

**Delroy:** From the French meaning belonging 'to the king'.

**Demetrius:** From the Greek meaning 'of Demeter', the goddess of agricultural fertility. Short spellings: Demetri, Dimitri.

**Dempsey:** From the Middle English meaning 'absence of merit', 'deserving of blame'.

**Denholm:** Possibly from the Scottish meaning 'place' or 'island valley'.

**Denis:** See Dionysus. Alternative spelling: Dennis, Dennes, Dennys. Short forms: Den, Denny.

**Denzil:** Possibly from the Celtic meaning 'stronghold' or the Old Cornish meaning 'high'. Alternative spelling: Denzel.

**Derek:** From the Old German meaning the people's ruler. Alternative spellings: Darrick, Dereck, Dirk.

**Dermot:** From the Irish meaning 'free from envy'. Alternative spellings: Diarmid, Diarmuid:

**Derry:** From the Welsh meaning 'oak trees' or the Irish Gaelic meaning 'red-haired'.

**Derwent:** From the Celtic meaning 'clear water'.

**Desi:** From the Latin meaning 'the desired one'.

**Desmond:** From the Latin *mundus* meaning 'the universe', 'the heavens', 'the skies', 'the earth' or 'mankind'.

**Dev:** From the Sanskrit meaning 'god'.

**Devlin:** From the Irish meaning 'misfortune'.

**Devon:** From the English county.

**Dewey:** From the Welsh meaning 'beloved'. Alternative spelling: Dewi.

**Dewi:** See David or Dewey.

**DeWitt:** From the Flemish meaning 'blonde'.

**Dexter:** From the Latin meaning 'right-handed'. Short form: Dex.

**Deyla:** From the Norse meaning 'compassionate'.

**Diarmuid:** See Dermot. Alternative spelling: Diarmid.

**Didier:** From the Latin meaning 'desired'. Short form: Didi.

**Diego:** See James.

**Dieter:** From the German meaning 'army of the people'.

**Dietrich:** From the German meaning 'people of wealth, power and riches'. Alternative spelling: Dedrick, Dedrik, Dieter, Dietz.

**Digby:** From the Old French meaning 'to make a dyke or ditch'.

**Diggory:** Possibly from the French meaning 'strayed,' 'lost'.

**Dillon:** From the Irish Gaelic meaning 'faithful'. Alternative spelling: Dilan, Dillen, Dylan.

**Dimitri:** See Demetrius.

**Dino:** From the German meaning 'little sword'; see also Dean.

**Dinsdale:** From the Irish Gaelic meaning 'settlement surround by a moat'.

**Dinsmore:** From the Irish Gaelic meaning 'fortified hill'.

**Dionysus:** From the Greek god of wine. Alternative spellings:

Denis, Dennes, Dionis, Dioniso, Dwight. Short forms: Den, Dio, Dion, Denny.

**Dirk**: See Derek.

**Dixon**: See Richard.

**Dodi**: From the Hebrew meaning 'beloved'. Alternative spelling: Dodo.

**Dolan**: From the Irish meaning 'dark-haired'.

**Dolph**: See Randolph.

**Dominic**: From the Latin *dominicus* meaning 'belong to a lord or master' or 'servant of God'. Alternative spellings: Domenic, Domenico, Dominik, Dominique, Domingo. Short forms: Dom, Don, Nic, Nick, Nickie, Nicky.

**Donahue**: From the Irish Gaelic meaning 'dark warrior'.

**Donal**: From the Gaelic meaning 'world mighty'.

**Donald**: From the Celtic name Domhnall meaning 'world' or 'mighty'. Alternative spelling: Donaldo. Short forms: Don, Donal, Doni, Donnie, Donny.

**Donatus**: From the Latin meaning 'given', 'bestowed upon'. Alternative spellings: Donat, Donato. Short forms: Don, Doni, Donnie, Donny.

**Donnel**: From the Gaelic meaning 'hill' or 'hill-fort'.

**Donnelly**: From the Celtic meaning 'brave' or 'dark/black man'.

**Donovan**: From the Celtic meaning 'dark' or 'brown-haired warrior'. Alternative spellings: Donovon. Short forms: Don,

Donnie, Donny, Van.

**Doran**: From the Greek *doron* meaning 'gift'. Alternative spellings: Doron, Dorian, Dore, Dorran.

**Dorek**: From the Polish meaning 'God's gift'.

**Dorian**: From the Greek dorios meaning 'child of the sea'; see also Doran.

**Dorran**: From the Celtic meaning 'strange' or the Greek meaning 'a gift'; see also Doran.

**Doug**: See Dougal or Douglas.

**Dougal**: From the Celtic name Dugald meaning 'dark stranger'. Short form: Doug.

**Douglas**: From the Celtic meaning 'dark water', 'dark stream'. Short form: Doug.

**Dov**: From the Hebrew meaning 'bear'; see also David.

**Doyle**: From the Irish meaning 'assembly', 'gathering'.

**Drake**: From the Gaelic meaning 'dragon' or the Greek meaning 'serpent'.

**Drew**: See Andrew.

**Driscoll**: From the Celtic meaning 'sad', 'distressed'.

**Druhan**: See Andrew.

**Dryden**: From the Middle English meaning 'dry secluded valley'.

**Duane**: From the Gaelic meaning 'black', 'dark'. Alternative spellings: Duayne, Dwane, Dwayne.

**Dudley**: From the Old English meaning 'Dudo's meadow'.

**Dugald**: From the Scottish meaning 'black stranger'.

**Dugan**: From the Irish Gaelic meaning 'small and dark'.

**Duke**: From the Latin dux meaning 'leader', 'conductor', 'guide', 'commander'.

**Dumont**: From the French meaning 'from the mountain/hill'.

**Duncan**: From the Celtic meaning 'brown warrior', 'dark-skinned warrior'.

**Dunstan**: From the Old English meaning 'greyish-brown fortress'.

**Durand**: From the Latin meaning 'to last', 'to endure'.

**Dustin**: From the Old German meaning 'fighter' or the Old Norse meaning 'Thor's stone'. Short forms: Dust, Dustie, Dusty.

**Dwight**: From the Old English or Old Dutch meaning 'white', 'fair' or the French version of 'Dionysis'.

**Dyfan**: From the Welsh meaning 'ruler of a tribe'.

**Dylan**: From the Welsh meaning 'son of the waves'. Alternative spelling: Dillon.

## E

**Eagan**: From the Irish meaning 'fiery', 'forceful'. Alternative spellings: Egan, Egon.

**Eamonn**: An Irish derivative of Edmund. Alternative spelling: Eamon.

**Earl**: From the Old English meaning 'nobleman' or 'chief'. Alternative spelling: Errol.

**Earnest**: See Ernest.

**Eben**: From the Hebrew meaning 'rock', 'stone'.

**Ebenezer**: From the Hebrew meaning 'stone of help' or 'foundation stone'.

**Eberhard**: From the Old German meaning 'courageous as a boar'.

**Ebner**: See Abner.

**Ed**: See Edgar, Edmund, Edward or Edwin.

**Edan**: From the Celtic meaning 'flame', 'fire'.

**Eden**: From the Hebrew meaning 'delight'.

**Edgar**: From the Old English meaning 'happy spear'. Alternative spelling: Adair. Short forms: Ed, Eddie, Eddy.

**Edison**: From the English meaning 'son of Edward'. Alternative spelling: Edson.

**Edmund**: From the Old English meaning 'happy protection' or 'happy guardian'. Alternative spellings: Eamon, Eamonn, Edmond, Edmondo, Edmundo. Short forms: Ed, Ned, Neddie, Ted, Teddy.

**Edoardo**: See Edward.

**Edom**: From the Hebrew meaning 'red'.

**Edric**: From the Old English meaning 'happy /prosperous ruler'.

**Edson**: See Edison.

**Edryd**: From the Welsh meaning 'restoration'.

**Edward**: From the Old English meaning 'rich guardian' or 'happy protector'. Alternative spellings: Edoardo, Edorta, Edouard,

Eduard, Eduardo, Edvard, Edvardo, Edwardo. Short forms: Ed, Eddie, Eddy, Edo, Edwy, Ned, Neddy, Ted, Teddy.

**Edwin**: From the Old English meaning 'rich friend'. Short form: Ed.

**Egan:** From the Irish Gaelic meaning 'small fiery one'.

**Egbert:** From the English meaning 'shining sword', 'bright sword'.

**Egerton**: From the Middle English meaning 'corner of the town' or the English meaning 'Edgar's town'.

**Egmont**: From the Middle English meaning 'corner of the hill'.

**Egor**: See George or Igor.

**Eifion**: From the Welsh meaning 'place name'.

**Eilir**: From the Welsh meaning 'butterfly'.

**Einar:** From the Old Norse meaning 'individualist' or 'lone warrior'.

**Eion**: See Ian.

**Elan**: From the Hebrew meaning 'tree' or the Latin meaning 'spirited'.

**Elazar**: From the Hebrew meaning 'God helped'. Alternative spelling: Eleazar.

**Eldon**: See Aldous.

**Eldwin**: See Aldwin.

**Eleazar**: From the Hebrew meaning 'God has helped'. Alternative spellings: Elazar, Elazaro, Elazer, Eliezer, Elizar.

**Elgar**: From the Old English meaning 'noble spear'.

**Elgin**: From the Old English *aethel* meaning 'noble' and the Celtic *gwen* meaning 'white', 'pure'.

**Eli**: From the Hebrew meaning 'height'. Alternative spelling: Ely.

**Elias**: See Elijah.

**Elihu**: See Eliyahu.

**Elijah**: From the Hebrew meaning 'faithful to God', 'the Lord is my God'. Alternative spellings: Elias, Ellis, Elliot. Short form: Eli.

**Elisha**: From the Hebrew meaning 'God is my help', 'God is generous'. Short form: Eli.

**Eliyahu**: From the Hebrew meaning 'the Lord is my God'. Alternative spelling: Elihu. Short form: Eli.

**Ellery**: From the English meaning 'elder tree island'.

**Elliot**: See Elijah.

**Ellis**: See Elijah.

**Ellison**: From the Old English meaning 'son of Ellis'.

**Elmer**: From the English meaning 'noble', 'famous'. Alternative spellings: Aylmer, Ellmer, Elmo.

**Elmo**: See Elmer or Erasmus.

**Elonzo**: See Alonzo.

**Eloy**: From the Latin meaning 'chosen one'.

**Elrad**: From the Old English meaning 'noble counsel'.

**Elroy**: From the Spanish meaning 'the king'.

**Elston**: From the Old English meaning 'the noble's town', or 'noble town'. Alternative spelling: Elton.

**Elton**: Possibly from the Old English meaning 'old town'; see also Elston.

**Elvin**: From the Old High German meaning 'elf-like', 'quick-witted' or 'clever friend'. Alternative spelling: Elvis.

**Elvis:** Possibly from the Scandinavian meaning 'wise' or the Old Norse meaning 'all-knowing'; see also Elvin.

**Elwyn:** From the Welsh meaning 'white brow'.

**Emanuel:** From the Hebrew meaning 'God is with us'. Alternative spelling: Emmanuel. Short forms: Manuel, Manu.

**Emerson:** From the German or English meaning 'son of Emery'.

**Emery:** From the Old High German meaning 'ruler', 'power' or 'wealth'. Alternative spellings: Almery, Amory, Emerick, Emerson, Emil, Emile, Emilio, Emlin, Emlyn, Emmerich, Emmerlich, Emory.

**Emil:** From the Latin meaning 'flatterer' or the German meaning 'industrious'. Alternative spellings: Emile, Émile, Emilek, Emiliano, Emilio, Emill, Emlyn.

**Emlyn:** See Emery or Emil.

**Emmanuel:** See Emanuel.

**Emmet:** From the Hebrew meaning 'truth'.

**Emory:** See Emery.

**Emrys:** From the Greek meaning 'immortal'.

**Emyr:** From the Welsh meaning 'honour'.

**Eneas:** See Aeneas.

**Engelbert:** From the Old German meaning 'bright as an angel'.

**Ennis:** From the Greek meaning 'mine'; see also Angus.

**Enoch:** From the Hebrew meaning 'dedicated' or 'educated'.

**Enos**: From the Hebrew meaning 'man'. Alternative spelling: Enosh.

**Enrique**: Spanish meaning 'ruler of a home' or 'estate/heir/person of a high rank'; see also Henry.

**Eoghan**: From the Gaelic meaning 'born of dew'; see also Eugene.

**Eoin**: See John.

**Erasmus**: From the Greek *erasmios* meaning 'loved', 'desired'. Short form: Elmo.

**Erhard**: From the Old German meaning 'resolution'.

**Eric**: From the Old Norse meaning 'sole ruler'. Alternative spellings: Eirik, Erik. Short forms: Rick, Ric.

**Erin**: From the Gaelic Éirinn meaning 'Ireland'. Alternative spelling: Ayrin.

**Ernest**: From the Old German meaning 'vigour' or 'earnestness'. Alternative spellings: Ernestino, Ernesto, Ernestus. Short forms: Ernie, Erno, Ernst.

**Ernie**: See Ernest.

**Ernst**: See Ernest.

**Errol**: From the Latin meaning 'wanderer'; see also Earl.

**Erskine**: From the Scottish meaning 'green ascent' or the Gaelic meaning 'from the height of the cliff'.

**Erwin**: From the Old English meaning 'sea friend'.

**Eryl**: From the Welsh meaning 'watcher'.

**Esau**: From the Hebrew meaning 'hairy'.

**Esmund**: From the Old English meaning 'very good' or 'gracious protector'. Alternative spelling: Esmond.

**Esteban**: See Stephen.

**Ethan**: From the Hebrew meaning 'constant', 'permanent', 'long-lived' or 'strong'. Alternative spelling: Etan.

**Ethelbert**: From the Old English name Aethelbryht from *aethel* meaning 'noble' and *beorht* meaning 'bright'.

**Ethelred**: From the Old English meaning 'noble strength'.

**Etienne**: See Stephen.

**Eugene**: From the Greek meaning 'well born'. Alternative spellings: Eoghan, Evgeny. Short form: Gene.

**Eunan**: From the Gaelic meaning 'great fear', 'little horror' or possibly from Adam.

**Eurig**: From the Welsh meaning 'gold'.

**Eustace**: From the Greek meaning 'rich in corn'. Short form: Stacey.

**Evan**: From the Irish meaning 'young warrior'; see also John. Alternative spellings: Ian, Euan, Ewan, Yves. Short form: Van.

**Evelyn**: From the Old English meaning 'hazelnut'.

**Everard**: From the Old High German meaning 'strong warrior'.

**Evgeny**: See Eugene.

**Ewan**: See Ewen or John.

**Ewen**: From the Irish name Eoghan meaning 'a youth'; see also John. Alternative spelling: Ewan.

**Ezekiel**: From the Hebrew meaning 'may God make strong'. Alternative spelling: Ezechial.

**Ezra:** From the Hebrew meaning 'help'. Alternative spellings: Esra, Ezer.

## F

**Fabian:** From the Latin meaning 'bean grower'. Alternative spellings: Fabien, Fabioano. Short forms: Fabio, Faber.

**Fabrizio:** From the Italian meaning 'craftsman'.

**Faine:** From the Old English meaning 'good-natured'. Alternative spelling: Fane.

**Falco:** From the German meaning 'people', 'tribe' or the Latin meaning 'falconer'. Alternative spellings: Falk, Falke, Falken.

**Farley:** From the Old English meaning 'fair meadow'.

**Farquhar:** From the Gaelic meaning 'friendly man'.

**Farran:** From the Irish meaning 'the land'.

**Faust:** From the Latin meaning 'lucky', 'fortunate'. Alternative spelling: Faustus.

**Favian:** From the Latin meaning 'understanding'.

**Federico:** From the Spanish or Italian meaning 'peaceful ruler'.

**Felipe:** The Spanish form of Philip.

**Felix:** From the Latin meaning 'happy'. Alternative spellings: Fela, Felex, Felic, Felicks, Felixiano.

**Fenn:** From the Old English meaning 'marsh'.

**Fergal:** From the Irish meaning 'man of strength'.

**Fernando:** From the Spanish meaning 'adventurer'. Alternative spelling: Fernand.

**Ferris:** The Irish Gaelic form of Peter.

**Festus:** From the German meaning 'festive', 'joyful', 'merry'.

**Finan:** From the Irish Gaelic meaning 'little and fair'. Alternative spelling: Finian.

**Finaly:** From the Scottish meaning 'fair hero'.

**Finbar:** From the Gaelic meaning 'fair head'.

**Fingal:** From the Gaelic meaning 'fair stranger'.

**Finlay:** From the Gaelic meaning 'a sunbeam' or 'small, fair-haired brave one'. Alternative spellings: Findlay, Findley, Finley. Short forms: Fin, Finn.

**Finn:** From the Gaelic meaning 'fair'; see also Finlay.

**Finnian:** From the Gaelic meaning 'fair'. Alternative spelling: Finnigan.

**Fintan:** From the Old Irish meaning 'white', 'fair' or possibly 'brave'. Alternative spelling: Fiontan.

**Fisk:** From the German meaning 'fish'.

**Fitz:** From the Old English meaning 'son'.

**Flavio:** From the Latin meaning 'blonde' or 'tawny'.

**Florian:** From the Slavic or Latin meaning 'flower'.

**Floyd:** See Lloyd.

**Flynn:** From the Irish meaning 'son of a red-haired man'. Alternative spellings: Flin, Flinn, Flyn.

**Fonzie:** See Alphonso.

**Ford**: From the English meaning 'shallow place to cross water'.

**Forrest**: From the Middle English meaning 'forest protector'.

**Foster**: From the English meaning 'forest ranger'.

**Francesco**: See Francis.

**Francis**: From the Latin meaning 'free man' or 'Frenchman'. Alternative spellings: Francesco, Francisco, Francois, Pancho, Paquito. Short forms: Frank, Franc, Frankie, Franky, Frans.

**François**: See Francis.

**Frank**: From the English meaning 'freeman' or possibly from fourth-century tribe that migrated to Gaul, meaning 'Frenchman'. Short forms: Franki, Frankie, Franky.

**Franklin**: From the English meaning 'landholder', 'freeman'. Alternative spelling: Franklyn.Short form: Frank.

**Fraser**: From the Old English meaning 'curly-haired' or the Old French meaning 'strawberry'. Alternative spellings: Fraiser, Frazer, Frazier.

**Fred**: Short form of names containing 'fred' such as Frederick and Alfred.

**Frederick**: From the Old German meaning 'peaceful ruler'. Alternative spellings: Fredrick, Friedrich, Fritz, Federico. Short forms: Fred, Freddie, Freddy, Ric, Rick, Rickie, Ricky.

**Fremont**: From the French meaning 'noble protector'.

**Frode**: From the Norwegian meaning 'wise'.

**Fyodor**: See Theodore.

## G

**Gabriel**: From the Hebrew meaning 'man of God', 'God's able-bodied one'. Alternative spellings: Gabrial, Gabriele, Gabrielle. Short forms: Gab, Gabby, Gabe, Gabie, Gabor.

**Gaelen**: From the Greek *galene* meaning 'calm', 'tranquil', 'healer' or 'peace' or the Gaelic meaning 'little bright one'. Alternative spellings: Gallen, Galen.

**Galvin**: From the Irish meaning 'sparrow'.

**Gareth**: From the Welsh meaning 'gentle'.

**Garfield**: From the Old English meaning 'spearfield'.

**Garnet**: From the French meaning 'keeper of the grain'.

**Garnett**: From the Latin meaning 'pomegranate seed' or the English meaning 'armed with a spear'.

**Garet**: From the French meaning 'to observe'.

**Garrett**: The Irish form of Gerard. Alternative spellings: Garet, Garett, Garritt, Gerrit.

**Garrick**: From the Old German meaning 'spear ruler' or the English meaning 'oak spear'. Alternative spellings: Garek, Garick, Garik, Garreck, Gerreck, Gerrik.

**Garth**: From the Scandinavian meaning 'garden' or the Old Norse meaning 'enclosure', 'from the garden' or 'protection'.

**Gary**: From the Old English *gar* meaning 'spear' or *gari* meaning 'spear man'. Alternative spelling: Garry.

**Gaspar**: See Caspar.

**Gavin**: From the Welsh meaning 'hawk of the plain' or 'white hawk'. Alternative spellings: Gauvin, Gawain, Gawaine, Gawin.

**Gene**: See Eugene.

**Geoffrey**: From the Old German meaning 'district' or 'peace' or the English meaning 'peaceful'. Alternative spellings: Geffrey, Godfrey, Gottfried, Jefferies, Jeffrey, Jefferson, Jeffries, Jefry, Jeffy. Short forms: Geoff, Jeff.

**George**: From the Greek meaning 'farmer'. Alternative spellings: Egor, Georg, Georges, Georgi, Georgie, Goran, Igor, Jorge, Jorn, Juergen, Jurgen, Yorick, Yuri.

**Geraint**: From the Welsh or Greek meaning 'old'.

**Gerald**: From the Old German meaning 'spear brave', 'spear strong' or 'warrior'. Aternative spelling: Jerald. Short forms: Gerry, Jerry.

**Gerard**: From the Old German meaning 'spear hard' or 'rules by the spear'. Alternative spellings: Garrad, Garrick, Garrett, Gearard, Geraint, Gerardo, Gerhard, Gerrard, Jerrald, Jerrold. Short forms: Garry, Gerry, Jerry.

**Gerlad**: From the Welsh meaning 'unknown'.

**Germaine**: See Jermaine.

**Gerry**: See Gerald or Gerard.

**Gervais**: From the Old German meaning 'spearman' or possibly from the French meaning 'honourable'. Alternative spelling:

Garvaise, Gervaise, Jarvis.

**Gethin**: From the Welsh meaning 'dusky'.

**Gideon**: From the Hebrew meaning 'cutter', 'one who cuts down'.

**Gilbert**: From the Old German meaning 'bright lad' or 'a famous or bright pledge'. Short forms: Gil, Bert, Bertie, Burt.

**Gilchrist**: From the Gaelic meaning 'servant of Christ'.

**Giles**: From the Greek meaning 'young shield', 'cripple', 'kid goat' or 'goat skin'.

**Giovanni**: The Italian form of John.

**Glen**: From the Welsh meaning 'from the valley'. Alternative spellings: Glenn, Glennard, Glyn, Glynn.

**Glyndwr**: From the Welsh meaning 'family name'.

**Godfrey**: From the Old German meaning 'God's peace'. Alternative spelling: Gottfried.

**Gordon**: From the Old English or Scottish meaning 'from the marshes' or 'small wooded dell marsh'.

**Graham**: From the Scottish meaning 'farm home'; the Greek meaning old or the Latin meaning 'grain'.

**Grant**: From the English or Scottish meaning 'bestow', 'great' or 'tall' or the Old French *granter* meaning 'to agree'.

**Gregory**: From the Greek meaning 'watchman'. Alternative spellings: Greggory, Gregor, Gregori, Gregorio, Grigor. Short forms: Greg, Gregg.

**Griffin**: From the Welsh meaning 'fighting chief' or 'fierce' or possibly from the Welsh name Gruffydd meaning 'lord'. Alternative spellings: Griffen, Gryphon. Short form: Griff.

**Griffith:** From the Welsh meaning 'reddish'.

**Gruffyd:** From the Welsh meaning 'powerful chief' or 'lord'.

**Guy:** From the Welsh meaning 'lively' or the German meaning 'wood' or 'wide'. Alternative spelling: Guido.

**Gwayne:** From the Welsh meaning 'white hawk'.

**Gwyn:** From the Welsh meaning 'fair blessed' or 'white'.

**Gywnfor:** From the Welsh meaning 'fair lord'.

## H

**Hadrian:** See Adrian.

**Hamish:** The Gaelic form of James.

**Hans:** See John.

**Hamlet:** From the Old English meaning 'small village'.

**Hanif:** From the Arabic meaning 'true believer'.

**Harley:** From the Middle Low German meaning 'hemp field'.

**Harrison:** From the Old English meaning 'son of Harry'.

**Harold:** From the Old Norse meaning 'army power', 'leader' or commander of an army' or the Old German meaning 'leader of an army'.

**Harry:** See Henry.

**Harvey:** From the French meaning 'battleworthy'.

**Hasan:** From the Arabic meaning 'handsome' or 'good'.

Alternative spellings: Hassan, Hussain, Hussein.

**Hayden**: From the Old English meaning 'pasture land'. Alternative spelling: Haydn.

**Heathcliff**: From the English meaning 'cliff near the heath'. Short forms: Heath, Cliff.

**Hector**: From the Greek meaning 'hold fast' or 'anchor'.

**Helmut**: From the Old French meaning 'strong defensive cover for the head' or 'helmet'.

**Henry**: From the Old German meaning 'ruler of the house'. Alternative spellings: Enrico, Enrique, Enzio, Ezio, Hedrick, Heindrick, Heinrich, Heinrick, Heinrik, Heinz, Hendrick, Henny, Henri, Henric, Henrik. Short forms: Hal, Hank, Harry, Rick, Rik.

**Herbert**: From the Old German meaning 'bright army'.

**Hesketh**: From the Norse meaning 'race course'.

**Hew**: See Hugh.

**Hilary**: From the Latin meaning 'cheerful'. Alternative spellings: Hillary, Hillery, Hilery. Short forms: Hilly, Hill.

**Hiram**: From the Hebrew meaning 'noble brother'.

**Holden**: From the English meaning 'sheltered place' or 'one who keeps watch'.

**Homer**: From the Greek meaning 'being hostage/led' or 'blind man'.

**Horace**: Possibly from the Latin meaning 'time' or 'hour'.

**Horatio**: From the Latin meaning 'punctual'. Alternative spellings:

Horacio, Horatius.

**Hosea**: From the Hebrew meaning 'salvation'.

**Howard**: Possibly from the Old English meaning 'hog-warden' or 'guardian of an enclosure'.

**Hubert**: From the Old German meaning 'bright mind'.

**Hugh**: From the Old German meaning 'bright mind', 'intelligent' or 'noble spirited'. Alternative spelling: Hew, Huw.

**Humphrey**: From the Old English meaning 'giant peace' or the Old German meaning 'strength of peace'.

**Huw**: The Welsh form of Hugh.

## I

**Ian**: The Scottish form of John; see also Ieuan. Alternative spellings: Iain, Ifan, Iwan, Eion, Ewan.

**Iestyn**: See Justin.

**Ieuan**: The Welsh form of John. Alternative spellings: Ian, Iain, Ifan, Iwan, Ewan.

**Ignatius**: From the Greek meaning 'fire'. Alternative spellings: Ignacius, Ignatz, Ignazio, Inigo. Short form: Iggy.

**Igor**: The Russian form of George. Alternative spelling: Egor.

**Ingmar**: From the Norse meaning 'famous son'.

**Innes**: From the Gaelic meaning 'island'.

**Iolo**: From the Welsh meaning 'lord value', 'worthy lord'.

**Ira**: From the Hebrew meaning 'watchful'.

**Irvine**: From the Scottish place name, or from the Gaelic meaning 'fair' or 'handsome'. Alternative spellings: Irvin, Irving.

**Irwin**: From the Old English meaning 'boar' and 'friend'.

**Isaac**: From the Hebrew meaning 'laughter'. Alternative spellings: Izaak. Short forms: Ike, Zak.

**Isaiah**: From the Hebrew meaning 'salvation of the Lord'. Short forms: Isa, Issah, Izzie.

**Ishmael**: From the Hebrew meaning 'God hears' or 'outcast'. Alternative spelling: Ismael.

**Isidore**: From the Greek meaning 'gift of Isis'.

**Israel**: From the Hebrew meaning 'he who strives with God' or 'may God prevail'.

**Istvan**: See Stephen.

**Ivan**: The Belorussian or Ukraninan version of John. Short forms: Ivo, Van.

**Ivo**: From the German meaning 'yew wood' or 'bow wood'; see also Ivan. Alternative spelling: Yves.

**Ivor**: From the Old Norse *ýr* meaning 'bow' and *herr* meaning 'warrior'; the Welsh meaning 'Lord' or the Latin word *ibor* meaning 'ivory'. Alternative spelling: Ifor. Short form: Ivo.

## J

**Jack**: See John.

**Jackson**: From the Old English meaning 'son of Jack'.

**Jacob**: From the Hebrew meaning 'deceiver' or 'supplanter'. Alternative spellings: Jakob, James, Yakov, Jacques, Jago. Short forms: Jake, Jackie.

**Jago**: See James.

**Jake**: See Jacob.

**James**: From the Hebrew meaning 'supplanter'. Alternative spellings: Diego, Hamish, Jago, Seamus. Short forms: Jamie, Jaime, Jim, Jimbo, Jimmie, Jimmy.

**Jameson**: From the English or Celtic meaning 'son of James'.

**Jared**: From the Hebrew meaning 'descent' or 'descending'. Atternative spelling: Jarod.

**Jarvis**: French variant of Gervaise meaning 'spearman'.

**Jason**: From the Greek meaning 'healer' or 'to heal'.

**Jasper**: From the Persian meaning 'treasure holder' or the French meaning 'green ornamental stone'. Alternative spellings: Caspar, Casper, Gaspar, Kaspa.

**Javier**: From the Spanish or Portuguese meaning 'bright'. Alternative spelling: Xavier.

**Jay**: Short form of most names beginning with J, now a name in its own right; also from the Latin *gaius* meaing 'jay', as in the bird.

**Jean**: See John.

**Jed**: From the Hebrew meaning 'friend of the Lord' or the Arabic *yed* meaning 'hand'.

**Jediah**: From the Hebrew meaning 'God knows'.

**Jedidiah**: From the Hebrew meaning 'Beloved of Jehovah'. Short form: Jed.

**Jeffrey**: See Geoffrey. Alternative spellings: Jeffery, Jeffory. Short form: Jeff.

**Jerald**: See Gerald.

**Jeremiah**: From the Hebrew meaning 'God exalts', 'God is on high'. Short forms: Jerry, Jeremy.

**Jeremy**: See Jeremiah. Short forms: Jerry, Jem, Jemmy.

**Jermaine**: From the Latin meaning 'brotherly'. Alternative spellings: Germaine.

**Jerome**: From the Greek name Hieronymus meaning 'holy name'.

**Jesse**: From the Hebrew meaning 'God exists', 'gift' or 'wealthy one.'

**Jesus**: From the Aramaic meaning 'Saviour' or 'God is salvation'. Alternative spelling: Husus, Jesuso. Short form: Jesu.

**Jethro**: From the Hebrew meaning 'abundance' or 'overflowing'.

**Joachim**: From the Hebrew meaning 'established by God'. Alternative spellings: Achim, Joaquin, Yackim.

**Joaquin**: See Joachim.

**Job**: From the Hebrew meaning 'persecuted', 'hated' or 'oppressed'.

**Joe**: See Joseph.

**Joel**: From the Hebrew meaning 'Jehovah is God' or 'God is willing'.

**John**: From the Hebrew meaning 'God is gracious'. Alternative spellings: Eoin, Euan, Evan, Ewan, Ewen, Giovanni, Hans, Ian, Ivan, Iwan, Iwen, Jack, Jago, Jan, Janos, Jay, Jean, Job, Jon,

Juan, Sean, Shane, Shaun, Shawn, Yves, Zane.

**Jonah**: From the Hebrew meaning 'dove'.

**Jonathon**: From the Hebrew meaning 'God has given'. Alternative spellings: Johnathan, Jonathan, Jonotan. Short forms: Jay, Jon, John, Johnny.

**Jordan**: From the Hebrew meaning 'flowing down'.

**Joseph**: From the Hebrew meaning 'God shall add'. Alternative spellings: Josef, Josephe, Joszef, Yusef. Short forms: Beppe, Beppi, Che, Chepe, Jody, Jodey, Joe, Joey, Pepe, Pepito, Pipo.

**Joshua**: From the Hebrew meaning 'God is my saviour'.

**Judah**: From the Hebrew meaning 'the praised one'. Short form: Jude.

**Jude**: See Judah.

**Julian**: From the Latin meaning 'belonging to Julius'. Short form: Jule, Jules, Julio.

**Justin**: From the Latin meaning 'righteous and just'. Alternative spelling: Iestyn. Short form: Just.

## K

**Kaelin**: From the Irish Gaelic name Caolán meaning 'slender'.

**Kai**: Possibly Welsh meaning 'man of the sea'.

**Kane**: From the Irish Gaelic meaning 'son of Cathan' or the Hebrew meaning either 'a spear', 'spear gatherer', 'a smithy' or 'possessed'. Alternative forms: Cahan, Cain.

**Kaspar:** See Jasper or Casper. Alternative spellings: Casper, Jaspar, Jasper, Kaspa, Kasper.

**Keegan:** From the Irish meaning 'little fiery one'.

**Keelin:** From the Gaelic meaning 'slender' and 'white' or possibly from the Irish Gaelic meaning 'mightly warrior'. Alternative spellings: Keely, Kellen.

**Keir:** From the Gaelic meaning 'of dark complexion'.

**Keith:** From the Gaelic meaning 'wood' or 'windy place'.

**Kelsey:** From the Old English *ceol* meaning 'ship' and *sige* meaning 'victory'.

**Kelvin:** Possibly from the Old English meaning 'water's friend' or the Scottish Gaelic meaning 'from the narrow stream'.

**Kendall:** From the Celtic meaning 'ruler of the valley'.

**Kenneth:** From the Gaelic meaning 'handsome'.

**Kevin:** From the Gaelic *caoimhín* meaning 'beloved'.

**Kieran:** From the Irish meaning 'little dark one'. Alternative spellings: Cieran, Cieron, Kieron. Short form: Kier.

**Kiernan:** Derived from the Irish *ciar* meaning 'black'. Alternative spelling: Kearnan.

**Kim:** From the Old English meaning 'royally bold'.

**Kirk:** From the Old Norse meaning 'church'.

**Kristofer:** See Christopher. Short form: Kris

**Kurt:** See Curtis.

**Kyle:** From the Gaelic *caol* meaning 'narrow'.

## L

**Lachlan**: From the Scottish Gaelic meaning 'fjord land' or 'land of the lakes'. Short forms: Lachie, Lochie.

**Lamar**: From the German meaning 'famous throughout the land' or the French meaning 'sea' or 'ocean'.

**Lamont**: From the Scandinavian meaning 'lawyer'. Alternative spelling: Lamond, Lamonte, Lammond.

**Lance**: From the Old German meaning 'land'; see also Lancelot. Alternative spelling: Launce.

**Lancelot**: From the Latin meaning 'lance' or the French meaning 'attendant'. Alternative spelling: Launcelot. Short forms: Lance, Launce.

**Lando**: Short form of Orlando.

**Larry**: See Laurence.

**Lars**: See Laurence.

**Larson**: See Laurence. Alternative spelling: Larsen.

**Larsen**: See Laurence.

**Laszlo**: From the Hungarian meaning 'famous ruler'. Alternative spellings: Laslo, Lazlo.

**Laurence**: From the Latin *lawrentium* meaning 'the place of the laurel trees' or 'laurel crowned'. Alternative spellings: Larsen, Larson, Laurencio, Laurens, Laurent, Lawrence, Lorenzo. Short forms: Lars, Larry, Larrie, Lauren, Laurie, Lorn, Lorne.

**Lawson**: From the English meaning 'son of Lawrence'.

**Leander**: From the Greek meaning 'brave as a lion' or 'lion man'. Alternative spelling: Leandro. Short forms: Leo, Lee, Lea.

**Lee**: From the Old English meaning 'meadow'; see also Leander. Alternative spelling: Leigh.

**Leif**: From the Scandinavian meaning 'beloved' or possibly 'son' or 'descendent'. Alternative spelling: Lief.

**Leigh**: See Lee.

**Leks**: See Alexander.

**Leland**: From the Old English meaning 'fallow land'.

**Lennart**: See Leonard.

**Lennon**: From the Gaelic Irish meaning 'small cloak' or 'cape'.

**Lennox**: From the Gaelic Scottish meaning 'with many elms'. Alternative spelling: Lenox.

**Leo**: From the Latin meaning 'lion'; see also Leonard or Leopold. Alternative spelling: Lev.

**Leolin**: See Llewelyn.

**Leon**: From the Latin meaning 'lion'.

**Leonard**: From the Old German meaning 'as strong as a lion'. Alternative spellings: Lennaert, Lennard, Leonardo, Leonart, Leonidas, Leonides. Short form: Len, Lenny, Leo.

**Leopold**: From the Old German meaning 'brave people'. Alternative spelling: Leopoldo. Short form: Leo.

**Leroy**: From the Old French meaning 'the king'.

**Leslie:** From the Scottish place name or from the Scottish Gaelic meaning 'grey fortress'. Alternative spelling: Leslee. Short forms: Lee, Les.

**Lester:** From the Latin meaning 'chosen camp' or from the English city Leicester. Short form: Les.

**Lestyn:** Welsh derivative from the Latin meaning 'just'.

**Lev:** From the Hebrew meaning 'heart' or the Russian form of Leo.

**Lewis:** See Louis, possibly also from the Celtic meaning 'lionlike'. Short form: Lew.

**Lex:** See Alexander.

**Liam:** The Irish form of William.

**Lindon:** See Lyndon.

**Lindsay:** From the Scottish family name of the Earls of Crawford or possibly from the Old English meaning 'linden tree island'. Alternative spellings: Lindsey, Linsey, Linsay.

**Linford:** From the Old English meaning 'linden-tree ford' or 'flax river crossing'. Alternative spelling: Lynford.

**Linley:** From the Old English meaning 'flax meadow'.

**Linus:** From the Greek meaning 'flaxen-haired' or 'net'.

**Lionel:** From the Latin meaning 'little lion' or 'lion cub'.

**Llew:** From the Welsh meaning 'lion'.

**Llewellyn:** From the Welsh meaning 'lionlike'. Alternative spellings: Leolin, Lewis, Llewelin, Llewellen, Llewelleyn, Llewellin, Llwellyn, Llywelyn.

**Lloyd**: From the Welsh meaning 'grey'. Alternative spelling: Floyd.

**Llyr**: From the Welsh originating from the ancient sea god Lear.

**Logan**: From the Scottish meaning 'low meadow' or possibly from the Scottish place of the same name in Ayrshire.

**Lon:** See Alphonse.

**Lonnie**: See Alphonse.

**Lorcan**: From the Irish meaning 'little' or 'fierce'.

**Lorenzo**: See Laurence.

**Lorne**: See Lawrence. Alternative spelling: Lorn.

**Lother**: See Luther.

**Lou:** See Louis.

**Louie**: See Louis.

**Louis**: From the German meaning 'famous warrior' or the French meaning 'famous'. Alternative spellings: Lewis, Ludwig, Ludovic, Luigi, Luis, Lutek. Short forms: Louie, Lou.

**Lovell**: From the French meaning 'wolf-cub'.

**Lucas**: From the Latin meaning 'light' or 'bringer of light' or possibly from the Latin meaning 'man from Lucania', a place in Southern Italy. Alternative spellings: Luckas, Lucus, Lukas. Short form: Luc, Luke.

**Lucian**: See Lucius.

**Lucien**: See Lucius.

**Lucius**: See Lucas. Alternative spellings: Lucian, Lucien, Lucio. Short forms: Luc, Luca, Lukas, Luke.

**Ludolf:** From the Old German meaning 'famous wolf'.

**Ludwig:** See Louis. Alternative spellings: Ludovic, Ludovico, Ludvig.

**Luigi:** See Louis.

**Luis:** See Louis.

**Lukas:** See Lucius.

**Luka:** See Lucius.

**Luke:** From the Greek *loukas* meaning 'man from Lucania'; see also Lucius or Lucas.

**Luther:** From the Old German meaning 'famous warrior'. Alternative spellings: Lothar, Lother, Luthor.

**Lyman:** From the Old English meaning 'man from the island'.

**Lyle:** From the French meaning 'islander' or possibly from the Scottish Gaelic meaning 'loyal'. Alternative spellings: Lyall, Lyell.

**Lyndon:** From the Old English meaning 'linden-tree hill'. Alternative spelling: Linden.

**Lysander:** From the Greek meaning 'liberator'. Short forms: Sander, Sandy.

## M

**Mac:** From the Scottish Gaelic meaning 'son'. Alternative spellings: Mack, Macke, Mackie.

**Macallister:** From the Scottish Gaelic meaning 'son of Alistair'.

**Macy**: From the French meaning 'Matthew's estate'.

**Maddock**: From the Welsh meaning 'generous'. Alternative spellings: Madoc, Madock, Madog.

**Maddox**: From the Welsh meaning 'benefactor's son'.

**Madison**: From the English meaning 'son of Maud' or 'good son'. Alternative spellings: Maddie, Maddison, Maddy, Madisson.

**Magnus**: From the Latin meaning 'great'.

**Magus**: From the Latin meaning 'learned man'.

**Mal**: See Malcolm.

**Malachi**: From the Hebrew meaning 'my messenger'.

**Malcolm**: From the Gaelic *maol Caluim* meaning 'servant of Columba'. Alternative spellings: Malcom, Malkolm, Calum, Callum, Kalum, Kallum. Short form: Mal.

**Malik**: From the Hebrew meaning 'reigning' or the Punjabi meaning 'lord' or 'master'.

**Mallory**: From the German meaning 'army counsellor'.

**Manasseh**: From the Hebrew meaning 'to forget'.

**Manfred**: From the Old English meaning 'man of peace'.

**Manuel**: See Emmanual.

**Marc**: See Marcus. Alternative spelling: Mark.

**Marcel**: See Marcus. Alternative spellings: Marcelo, Marchello, Marsello, Marselo.

**Marcellus**: See Marcus. Alternative spellings: Marceau, Marcel, Marcello, Marciano.

**Marcus**: From the Roman god of war, Mars. Alternative spellings: Marcel, Marcellus, Marcio, Marco, Marcos, Marek, Marius, Mark, Marko, Markov, Markus. Short form: Marc.

**Marian**: See Mark.

**Marin**: From the French meaning 'sailor'. Alternative spellings: Marino, Mario.

**Mario**: The Spanish form of Marius or from *maris* meaning 'male' or 'virile'.

**Marius**: See Marcus.

**Mark**: See Marcus. Alternative spellings: Marc, Marek, Marian, Mariano, Marko, Markos.

**Markus**: See Marcus.

**Marlon**: See Merlin.

**Marmaduke**: From the Irish meaning 'servant of Madoc'.

**Marquis**: From the French meaning 'nobleman' or 'ruler of the marches'. Alternative spelling: Marquess.

**Marshall**: From the Old French meaning 'groom'.

**Marti**: See Martin.

**Martin**: From the Latin meaning 'martial' or 'warlike' or a form of Martinus meaning 'belonging to Mars'. Alternative spellings: Marciano, Marius, Martan, Marten, Martine, Martino, Marton, Martyn, Morten. Short forms: Marti, Marty.

**Marvin**: From the English meaning 'lover of the sea' or 'famous friend'. Alternative spellings: Marwin, Marven, Mervin. Short form: Marv.

**Mason**: From the French meaning 'stone mason'.

**Massimo**: From the Italian meaning 'greatest'.

**Mateo**: See Matthew. Alternative spellings: Matteo, Matias.

**Matheu**: See Matthew.

**Mathias**: See Matthew. Alternative spellings: Matthais, Mathis, Matteus.

**Matthew**: From the Hebrew meaning 'gift of the Lord'. Alternative spellings: Maitia, Mateo, Matheu, Mathew, Mathias, Mathieu, Mathiew, Mathis, Mattek, Matthaus. Mattheus, Matthieu, Mattia, Mattias, Mattieux. Short forms: Mat, Mati, Matie, Matt, Mattie, Matty, Maty.

**Maurice**: From the Latin meaning 'dark-skinned' or the Greek meaning 'Moor'. Alternative spellings: Maruin, Mauricio, Maurio, Mauritz, Maury, Morice, Moris, Morrice, Morris.

**Max**: See Maximillian or Maxwell.

**Maxime**: From the French meaning 'most excellent'. Alternative spelling: Maxim.

**Maximillian**: From the Latin meaning 'greatest'. Alternative spellings: Massimilliano, Maxim, Maximilien, Maximilion, Maximo, Maximos. Short forms: Max, Maxie, Maxy, Milo.

**Maxwell**: From the English meaning 'great spring' or possibly the Scottish Gaelic meaning 'Mack's well'. Short forms: Max, Maxie, Maxy.

**Maynard**: From the English meaning 'powerful'.

**Mel:** See Melvin.

**Melech**: From the Hebrew meaning 'king'. Alternative spelling: Melek.

**Melfyn**: From the Welsh meaning 'from Camarthen'.

**Melvin**: From the Celtic meaning 'chief' or the Gaelic meaning 'smooth brow'. Alternative spellings: Melvino, Melvyn. Short form: Mel.

**Meredith**: From the Welsh meaning 'guardian of the sea' or 'great chief'. Alternative spellings: Merideth, Meridith, Meredyth. Short form: Merry.

**Merion**: From the Welsh place Merion; see also Merlin.

**Merle**: See Merlin or Merill; possibly also from the French meaning 'blackbird'.

**Merlin**: From the Welsh name Myrddin meaning 'sea fort'. Alternative spellings: Merion, Marlon, Merle, Merlen, Merlinn, Merlyn, Merlynn.

**Merrick**: From the English meaning 'ruler of the sea'. Alternative spellings: Mayrick, Merek, Meric, Merrik.

**Merrill**: From the Irish meaning 'bright sea' or the French meaning 'famous'. Alternative spellings: Meril, Merill, Merle, Merrel, Merrell, Merril, Meryl.

**Mervin**: From the Welsh Myrddin meaning 'sea hill'. Alternative spelling: Mervyn. Short form: Merv.

**Micah**: From the Hebrew meaning 'who is like Yahweh [God]'. Alternative spellings: Mica, Micaiah, Michiah, Mikah.

**Michael**: The Greek form of Micah. Alternative spellings: Michaele, Michail, Michal, Michale, Michel, Michele, Michelet, Mikael, Mitchell. Short forms: Mic, Mick, Micky, Miguel, Mihail, Mik, Mike, Mikey, Miki, Mikie, Mikki, Misha.

**Miguel**: See Michael.

**Mihail**: See Michael.

**Miles**: From the Old German meaning 'gentle' or possibly 'generous' or 'merciful'; the Latin meaning 'soldier' or the Greek meaning 'millstone'. Alternative spelling: Myles. Short form: Milo.

**Milton**: From the English meaning 'mill town'.

**Misha**: See Michael.

**Mishka**: From the Russian meaning 'little bear'.

**Mitch**: See Mitchell.

**Mitchell**: From the Middle English meaning 'Who is like God'; see also Michael. Short form: Mitch.

**Monroe**: From the Scottish meaning 'from the river's mouth' or 'wheel turner'. Alernative spellings: Monro, Munro, Munroe.

**Montgomery**: From the English meaning 'rich man's mountain' or 'mountain of one who rules'. Short form: Monty.

**Moray**: From the Celtic meaning 'sea'. Alternative spelling: Murray.

**Morcant**: From the Welsh meaning 'brilliant'.

**Mordechai**: From the Hebrew meaning 'martial' or 'warlike'. Alternative spelling: Mordecai. Short form: Morty, Mort.

**Mordred**: From the Latin meaning 'painful'.

**Morgan**: From the Welsh meaning 'sea dweller' or 'great' and 'bright'. Alternative spellings: Morgen, Morcant.

**Moris**: See Maurice.

**Morley**: From the English surname composed of mor meaning 'moor' and leah meaning 'wood' or 'clearing'.

**Morris**: See Maurice. Short forms: Moss, Morry.

**Mort**: See Morten, Mortimer, Morton.

**Morten**: See Martin. Short form: Mort.

**Mortimer**: From the French meaning 'still water'. Short forms: Mort, Morty.

**Morton**: From the English meaning 'town near the moor'. Short form: Mort.

**Morven**: From the Scottish meaning 'mariner'.

**Moses**: From the Hebrew meaning 'delivered' or the Eygptian meaning 'child' or 'son'. Alternative spellings: Moise, Moises, Moishe, Moyses. Short forms: Mo, Moe, Moss.

**Muir**: From the Scottish meaning 'moor'.

**Mungo**: From the Gaelic meaning 'amiable' or 'beloved'.

**Munro**: See Monroe.

**Murdoch**: From the Gaelic meaning 'mariner' or 'sea warrior'.

**Murphy**: From the Celtic *muir* meaning 'from the sea'.

**Murray**: From the Gaelic Scottish meaning 'from the sea'.

**Myron**: Possibly from the Greek meaning 'fragrant', 'myrrh' or 'sweet oil'.

## N

**Nahum**: From the Hebrew meaning 'consoling'.

**Nathan**: From the Hebrew meaning 'gift'. Short forms: Nat, Nate, Natal.

**Nathanael**: From the Hebrew meaning 'gift of God'. Alternative spellings: Nathaniel, Nataniel. Short forms: Nat, Nate, Natal, Nathan.

**Ned**: See Edward.

**Neil**: From the Irish Gaelic *niadh* meaning 'champion' or possibly from the Old Norse name Niel. Alternative spellings: Neal, Neale, Neill, Neils, Niall, Niel, Niels, Niles, Nils, Nilson.

**Nestor**: From the Greek meaning 'traveller', 'remember' or 'wise'.

**Nelson**: From the Old English meaning 'Neil's son'.

**Neville**: From the French *neuville* meaning 'new town'. Alternative spellings: Nevil, Nevill, Neven.

**Niall**: See Neil.

**Nicholas**: From the Greek meaning 'victory of the people'. Alternative spellings: Nicolas, Nikolai, Nikolas, Nikolaus, Nikolos. Short forms: Colin, Claus, Klaus, Nic, Nick, Nicky, Nickie, Nico, Nicol,

Nicoll, Nicolai, Nik, Niki, Nikki, Niko, Nilo.

**Nigel**: From the Irish Gaelic meaning 'champion'; the Latin *nigellus* meaning 'black', 'dark' or the Old English meaning 'night'. Short forms: Nige, Nye.

**Nikodémus**: From the Greek *nike* meaning 'victory' and *demos* meaning 'population'.

**Noah**: From the Hebrew meaning 'rest'. Alternative spelling: Noach.

**Noam**: From the Hebrew meaning 'pleasantness'.

**Noël**: From the French meaning 'Christ's birthday'.

**Nolan**: From the Celtic meaning 'famous' or 'noble' or possibly from the Irish meaning 'shout'. Alternative spelling: Nolen.

**Norbert**: From the Old English meaning 'bright North'.

**Norman**: From the Old English meaning 'man from the North'.

**Norris**: From the Old English meaning 'northerner'.

## O

**Oberon**: From the German meaning 'noble' or 'bearlike'.

**Octavio**: From the Latin meaning 'eighth'. Alternative spelling: Octave.

**Odell**: From the Greek meaning 'ode' or 'melody'; the Irish meaning 'otter' or the English meaning 'forested hill'.

**Odo**: From the Old English *ead* meaning 'rich'.

**Ogden**: From the Old English meaning 'oak tree valley'.

**Olav:** From the Old Norse meaning 'ancestor'. Alternative spelling: Olaf.

**Oleg:** From the Russian meaning 'holy'.

**Oliver:** From the French meaning 'olive tree'. Alternative spelling: Olivier, Oliviero. Short forms: Oli, Olli, Olly.

**Omar:** From the Arabic meaning 'eloquent', 'highest' or 'long life'.

**Oran:** From the Irish Gaelic meaning 'green'.

**Oren:** From the Hebrew meaning 'pine tree'.

**Orlando:** From the German or Spanish meaning 'famous throughout the land'; see also Roland. Alternative spellings: Olando, Orland, Orlanda, Orlandus, Orlondo. Short forms: Lando, Olo, Orlan, Orlo.

**Orson:** From the Latin meaning 'bear'.

**Orville:** From the French meaning 'gold town'.

**Oscar:** From the Old English meaning 'divine spear'. Alternative spelling: Oskar.

**Osmond:** From the Old English meaning 'protected by God'. Alternative spellings: Åsmund, Osmand, Osmund, Osmundo. Short forms: Os, Ossie, Oz, Ozzie.

**Oswald:** From the Old English meaning 'divine power'. Alternative spellings: Osvaldo, Oswaldo, Oswold. Short forms: Os, Ossie, Oz, Ozzie.

**Otis:** From the Greek meaning 'keen of hearing'.

**Otto:** From the Old German meaning 'possessions'.

**Owain**: From the Welsh meaning 'well-born'. Alternative spellings: Owen.

**Oz**: From the Hebrew meaning 'strength'; see also Oswald.

## P

**Pablo**: See Paul.

**Padraig**: From Patrick meaning 'nobleman'.

**Paolo**: See Paul.

**Paris**: After the Greek mythological character who carried Helen off to Troy thus beginning the Trojan War or possibly from the Greek meaning 'lover'. Alternative spelling: Parris.

**Parish**: From the Greek meaning 'neighbour'.

**Parker**: From the English meaning 'park keeper'.

**Pascal**: From the French meaning 'Easter'. Alternative spellings: Pascoe, Pascual, Pasqual, Pasquale.

**Patrick**: From the Latin meaning 'noble'. Alternative spellings: Padraig, Padriac, Padrig, Patric, Patrice, Patricio, Peyton. Short forms: Paddy, Pat, Patsy.

**Paul**: From the Latin meaning 'small'. Alternative spellings: Pablo, Paolo, Paulo, Pavel.

**Percival**: From the French meaning 'penetrate the valley'. Alternative spellings: Perceval, Parsifal. Short forms: Percy, Perce.

**Peregrine**: From the Latin meaning 'traveller' or 'foreigner'. Short form: Perry.

**Peter**: From the Greek *petros* meaning 'stone' or 'rock'. Alternative spellings: Ferris, Pedro, Petros, Petter, Pierce, Pierre, Piers, Pieter. Short form: Pete.

**Peyton**: See Patrick.

**Phelan**: From the Irish meaning 'wolf'.

**Philip**: From the Greek meaning 'fond of horses'. Alternative spellings: Filip, Felipe, Felippe, Filippo, Philipp, Phillip, Phillipp. Short form: Phil, Pip.

**Phineas**: From the Hebrew meaning 'oracle'.

**Pierce**: From the Middle English form of Peter.

**Piers**: See Peter.

**Preston**: From the Old English meaning 'priest's statement' or 'priest's town'.

**Prince**: From the Latin meaning 'to take first place'.

**Prior**: From the Latin meaning 'the first'.

## Q

**Quentin**: From the Latin meaning 'fifth' or possibly from the English meaning 'Queen's town'. Alternative spellings: Quenton, Quintin, Quinton. Short forms: Quin, Quinn, Quinny.

**Quincy**: From the French meaning 'fifth son's estate'. Alternative spelling: Quincey. Short form: Quince.

**Quinlan**: From the Irish meaning 'strong' or 'well-shaped'.

**Quinn**: From the Irish meaning 'counsel'.

## R

**Rab**: See Robert.

**Rafferty**: From the Gaelic meaning 'rich and prosperous'. Short forms: Raf, Rafe. Raff.

**Rainer**: From the Old German meaning 'mighty army'. Alternative spelling: Raynor.

**Ralf**: From the Old English meaning 'wolf counsel' or 'fearless advisor'. Alternative spellings: Radolphus, Rafe, Ralph, Ralfie, Ralphael, Ralphel, Ralphie, Ralston, Raoul, Raul, Rolf.

**Ramon**: See Raymond.

**Ramsey**: From the English village or possibly from the Old English meaning 'sheep island'. Alternative spelling: Ramsay.

**Randall**: See Randolph.

**Randolph**: From the Old English meaning 'shield wolf' implying courageous protection. Alternative spellings: Randall, Randol, Randolf, Randolfo, Randolpho. Short forms: Randy, Dolph.

**Ralph**: See Ralf.

**Rapha**: From the Hebrew meaning 'he heals'. Alternative spelling: Rafer.

**Raphael**: From the Hebrew meaning 'God has healed'. Alternative spelling: Rafael, Rafaello. Short forms: Rafe, Rafi.

**Raymond**: From the Old English meaning 'protector' or

'guardian'. Alternative spellings: Raimond, Raimondo, Ramon, Ramond, Raymund, Redmond. Short form: Ray.

**Rayner**: From the Old German *ragan* meaning 'wisdom' or 'advice' and *harja* meaning 'army' or 'people' thus 'powerful army' or the Scandinvian meaning 'strong counsellor'. Alternative spelling: Ragnor, Rainer, Ranier, Raynor. Short form: Ray.

**Redmond**: See Raymond.

**Reece**: From the Welsh meaning 'ardent' or 'fiery'. Alternative spelling: Rhys.

**Regan**: From the Irish meaning 'descendant of the little king'. Alternative spellings: Reagan, Reagen.

**Reginald**: From the Old German meaning 'power force' or 'great warrior'. Alternative spellings: Ranald, Regnault, Reinald, Reinhold, Reinold, Reinwald, Renaldo, Renaud, Renault, Rene, Rex. Short forms: Reg, Reggie.

**Reid**: From the Old English read meaning 'red'.

**Reilly**: From the Irish meaning 'valiant'.

**Reuben**: From the Hebrew meaning 'behold a son'. Alternative spellings: Ruben, Reuven, Rouvin.

**Rex**: From the Latin meaning 'king'; see also Reginald.

**Reinhold**: From the German *ragin* meaning 'advice' and *wald* meaning 'ruler'. Alternative spellings: Reynold, Rheinhallt.

**Reynard**: From the Old German meaning 'wise, strong', 'bold', 'brave'. Alternative spellings: Rheinhallt, Renard, Renart, Renaud, Renke, Reynaud, Reynauld, Reyner, Reynold. Short form: Rey.

**Rhett**: See Rhys.

**Rhodri**: From the Welsh meaning 'circle ruler' or 'crowned ruler'.

**Rhodric**: From the Greek and Old English meaning 'fine and caring ruler'.

**Rhys**: From the Welsh meaning 'ardour' or 'rashness'. Alternative spellings: Reese, Rhett.

**Richard**: From the Old German meaning 'strong ruler'. Alternative spellings: Ricardo, Riccardo, Richardo, Richart. Short forms: Dick, Dickie, Dicky, Dixon, Rich, Richie, Rick, Ricky.

**Ridley**: From the Old English meaning 'meadow of reeds'.

**Riley**: From the English meaning 'rye'. Alternative spelling: Reilly.

**Riordan**: From the Gaelic meaning 'poet king'.

**Roald**: From the Scandinavian meaning 'renowned' or 'powerful'.

**Robert**: From the Old German *hrod* meaning 'fame' and *berht* meaning 'bright'. Alternative spellings: Robard, Roban, Robin, Rupert. Short forms: Bob, Bobbie, Bobby, Rab, Rob, Robbie, Robby.

**Robin**: See Robert. Alternative spelling: Robyn.

**Roderick**: From the Old German meaning 'famous ruler'. Alternative spellings: Roderic, Roderich, Roderigo, Rodrigo, Rodrique, Rurik. Short forms: Rod, Rodd, Roddy, Rori, Roric,

Rory, Ruy.

**Rodney**: From the Old English meaning 'reed island'. Short forms: Rod, Rodd, Roddy.

**Roger**: From the Old German meaning 'famous spear', 'renowned warrior'. Alternative spellings: Rodger, Rudiger, Ruggerio, Rutger, Ruttger.

**Roland**: From the Old German meaning 'famous land'. Alternative spellings: Rolando, Rollan, Rolland, Rowland, Orlando. Short form: Rollo.

**Rolf**: From the Old German meaning 'famous wolf'.

**Rollo**: See Roland.

**Romain**: From the Latin meaning 'citizen of Rome'.

**Ronald**: From the Norse name Rögnvaldr meaning 'decisive ruler'. Alternative spellings: Ranald, Roald. Short forms: Ron, Roni, Ronnie, Ronny.

**Ronan**: From the Irish meaning 'little seal'. Alternative spelling: Rowan.

**Rory**: From the Gaelic meaning 'red'; see also Roderick.

**Ross**: From Gaelic meaning 'peninsular'.

**Rowan**: From the Irish Gaelic meaning 'little red one'.

**Roy**: From the Gaelic meaning 'red'.

**Royce**: From the English meaning 'famous'.

**Royston**: From the English meaning 'red town'.

**Rudolf**: From the Old German meaning 'famous wolf' implying 'famous for boldness and courage'. Alternative spelling: Rudolph.

**Rudyard:** From the Saxon meaning 'red pole'.

**Rufus:** From the Latin meaning 'red-haired'.

**Rupert:** The German form of Robert. Alternative spelling: Ruprecht. Short form: Rupe.

**Russell:** From the French meaning 'a man with red hair'. Alternative spelling: Russel. Short form: Russ.

**Ryan:** From Irish meaning 'little king'. Alternative spellings: Rian, Rion, Ryen.

## S

**Salvador:** From the Latin meaning 'saviour'. Alternative spellings: Salvadore, Salvator, Salvatore.

**Samson:** From the Hebrew meaning 'child of the sun'.

**Samuel:** From the Hebrew meaning either 'heard by God' or 'requested by God'. Short forms: Sam, Sammy.

**Sanjay:** From the Sanskrit meaning 'triumphant'.

**Sasha:** See Alexander.

**Saul:** From the Hebrew meaning 'asked for'. Short forms: Solly, Sollie.

**Sava:** From the Greek meaning 'old man'. Alternative spelling: Savas.

**Saxon:** From the German meaning 'knife'.

**Sayer:** From Welsh origins meaning 'carpenter'.

**Scott**: From the Old English meaning 'man of Scotland'. Alternative spellings: Scot, Scottie, Scotty.

**Seamus**: See James or Jacob. Alternative spelling: Shamus.

**Sean**: See John.

**Sebastian**: From the Greek meaning 'venerable'. Alternative spelling: Sebastien. Short forms: Seb, Basti, Bastiano, Bastien.

**Selwyn**: From the Old English meaning 'blessed, valuable friend'.

**Seth**: From the Hebrew meaning 'appointed'.

**Seward**: From the Old English meaning 'of the sea'. Alternative spelling: Sayward.

**Seymour**: From the Old English meaning 'wild coastal land'.

**Shane**: See John. Alternative spellings: Shayne, Sean.

**Shawn**: See John.

**Shelly**: From the English meaning 'meadow on a slope'.

**Sherlock**: From the Old English meaning 'fair-headed' or possibly 'woodland'.

**Sidney**: From the Old English meaning 'wide, well-watered land' or 'meadow by the river'. Alternative spelling: Sydney. Short forms: Sid, Syd.

**Siegfried**: From the Old High German meaning 'peace after victory'. Alternative spelling: Sigfried.

**Sigmund**: From the German meaning 'victory'. Alternative spellings: Siegmond, Siegmund, Sigismund.

**Silas**: From the Greek meaning 'wide, well-watered land'; the

Hebrew meaning 'to borrow' or the Latin s*ilus* meaning 'snub-nosed' or *silva* meaning 'wood'; see also Silvan.

**Silvan**: From the Latin meaning 'wood' or 'forest dweller'. Short form: Silas.

**Silvester**: From the Latin meaning 'of the woods'. Alternative spellings: Sylvester, Sylvestro. Short form: Sly.

**Simon**: From the Greek meaning 'snub-nosed' or the Hebrew meaning 'he heard'. Alternative spellings: Shimon, Simeon, Simone. Short form: Si.

**Skye**: From the Scottish island.

**Sol**: From the Latin meaning 'sun'; see also Solomon.

**Solomon**: From the Hebrew meaning 'peace'. Short forms: Sol, Solly.

**Spencer**: From the Middle English meaning 'steward' or 'butler'.

**Spike**: From the Latin meaning 'point'.

**Spiro**: From the Greek meaning 'breath of life'.

**Stacey**: See Eustace.

**Stanislaus**: From the Slav meaning 'glory of the camp'. Alternative spellings: Stanislav, Stanislaw. Short form: Stan.

**Stanley**: From the Old English *stan* meaning 'stone' and *leah* meaning 'clearing'. Short form: Stan.

**Stefan**: See Stephen.

**Stephen**: From the Greek *stefanos* meaning 'garland' ,'crown' or 'wearer of the crown'. Alternative spellings: Esteban, Estes,

Etienne, Etiennes, Istvan, Stefan, Stefano, Steffan, Stevan, Steven. Short form: Steve.

**Sterling**: From the English meaning 'genuine' and 'reliable' or the Old English meaning 'star'. Alternative spelling: Stirling.

**Steven**: See Stephen.

**Stewart**: From the Old English meaning 'household servant'. Alternative spellings: Stuart, Steward. Short forms: Stew, Stewie, Stu.

**Stuart**: See Stewart.

**Sven**: From the Norse meaning 'boy'.

## T

**Taffy**: See David.

**Tarquin**: Unknown meaning, but possibly of Etruscan origins.

**Tate**: From the Middle English *tayt* meaning 'cheerful' or 'spirited'.

**Tavish**: From the Gaelic meaning 'twin'.

**Taylor**: From the Old English meaning 'tailor'.

**Ted**: See Edward or Theodore.

**Terence**: From the Latin meaning 'tender'. Alternative spellings: Terencio, Terrance, Terrence, Torrance, Torrence. Short form: Terry.

**Tevye**: From the Hebrew meaning 'man of goodness'. Alternative spellings: Tobias, Tuvia.

**Thaddeus**: See Theodore. Short form: Tad, Thad.

**Theobold:** From the Old German meaning 'brave people'. Short form: Theo.

**Theodore:** From the Greek meaning 'God's gift'. Alternative spellings: Fedor, Feodor, Fyodor, Teodore, Thaddaus, Thaddeus, Thadeus, That, Theodor. Short forms: Ted, Tedd, Teddie, Teddy, Teodor, Thad, Thaddy, Thady, Theo, Tod, Todd.

**Thomas:** From the Greek *didymos* meaning 'twin'. Alternative spelling: Tomas. Short forms: Tam, Thom, Thoma, Tom, Tommie, Tommy.

**Thurstan:** From the Old German meaning 'Thor's stone'.

**Tiger:** From the Greek *tigris* meaning 'tiger'.

**Timon:** Possibly from the Greek meaning 'honourable'.

**Timothy:** From the Greek meaning 'honouring God'. Short form: Tim, Timkin,Timmy, Timo.

**Titus:** Possibly from the Greek meaning 'day' or 'sun'. Short form: Tito.

**Tobias:** From the Hebrew meaning 'God is good'. Alternative spellings: Tobin Tobit, Tobyn. Short forms: Tobe, Tobey, Tobie, Toby.

**Toby:** See Tobias.

**Todd:** From the Middle English meaning 'fox'.

**Torcall:** From the Old Norse meaning 'Thor's cauldron'. Alternative spelling: Torquil.

**Travis:** From the English or French meaning 'to cross'.

**Tremayne:** From the English meaning 'town built of stone'.

**Trevor:** From the Irish Gaelic meaning 'wise' or the Welsh meaning 'large homestead' or 'Godly town'. Alternative spelling: Trefor.

**Tristan:** From the Celtic meaning 'tumult' or possibly from the Welsh name Tristram or the Old Welsh word *trys-tan* meaning 'noisy one'. Alternative spelling: Trystan.

**Troy:** From the old city in Asia Minor.

**Truman:** From the English meaning 'true man'.

**Tyler:** From the Old English meaning 'someone who tiles roofs'. Alternative spelling: Tylor.

**Tyrone:** From the Irish meaning 'Eoghan's land'.

**Tyson:** From the French meaning 'firebrand' or 'fiery'.

## U

**Ullrick:** From the Old English meaning 'powerful wolf' or 'powerful ruler'. Alternative spellings: Ullric, Ullrich, Ulric, Ulrich, Ulrick.

**Ulysses:** From the Greek name Odysseus. The meaning is uncertain though it possibly comes from the Latin meaning 'hateful'.

**Uriah:** From the Hebrew meaning 'my light is the Lord'. Alternative spelling: Uriel.

**Urien:** From the Welsh meaning 'privileged birth'.

## V

**Valentine**: From the Latin *valens* meaning 'to be strong'. Alternative spellings: Valencio, Valentino.

**Van**: See Evan or Ivan.

**Vance**: From the English meaning 'thresher' or 'someone who lives near a marsh'.

**Vaughan**: From the Welsh meaning 'little' or 'small'. Alternative spelling: Vaughn.

**Vernon**: From the French meaning 'alder tree' or 'alder grove' or the Latin meaning 'springlike' or 'youthful'. Short forms: Vern, Verne.

**Victor**: From the Latin meaning 'conqueror'. Alternative spellings: Victoire, Victorio, Viktor, Vittorio. Short form: Vic.

**Vincent**: From the Latin meaning 'to conquer'. Alternative spellings: Vincente, Vincenzo. Short forms: Vin, Vince, Vinnie, Vinny.

**Virgil**: From the Roman name Vergilius.

**Vivian**: From the Latin meaning 'alive'.

**Vladislav**: From the Polish *volod* meaning 'rule' and *slav* meaning 'glory'.

## W

**Wade**: From the English meaning 'ford'.

**Wallace**: From the Celtic meaning 'Welshman' or the Old French meaning 'foreign' or 'stranger'. Alternative spelling: Wallis. Short forms: Wal, Wally.

**Walter**: From the Old German meaning 'ruling people'. Alternative spellings: Walden, Waldo, Walther, Watkins. Short forms: Wal, Wally, Wat.

**Ward**: From the English meaning 'guardian' or 'watchman'.

**Warren**: From the Old German meaning 'guard'.

**Wayland**: From the Old English meaning 'land by the path'.

**Wayne**: From the Old English meaning 'wagon maker' or the Old English meaning 'meadow'.

**Wesley**: From the Old English meaning 'west meadow'.

**Weston**: From the Old English meaning 'west enclosure'.

**Wilber**: From the Old English meaning 'well', 'willow' or 'bright'. Alternative spelling: Wilbur. Short forms: Wil, Will, Willie, Willy.

**Wilbert**: From the Old English meaning 'well bright'. Short forms: Wil, Will, Willie, Willy.

**Wilfred**: From the Old English meaning 'resolute' or the Old English meaning 'wish for peace'. Alternative spelling: Wilfrid. Short forms: Wil, Will, Willie, Willy.

**Willard**: From the Old English meaning 'hardy and resolute'. Short forms: Wil, Will, Willie, Willy.

**William**: From the Old German meaning 'resolute protector'.

Alternative spellings: Guilaume, Guillaume, Liam, Quillermo, Vasilos, Vassos, Vilhelm, Welef, Wilhelm, Willem, Wilmer, Wilson. Short forms: Bill, Billy, Wil, Will, Willie, Willy.

**Wilmar:** From the Old German meaning 'famous'. Alternative spelling: Wilmer.

**Winfred:** From the Old English meaning 'friend'.

**Winston:** Named after the Gloucestershire village or possibly from the Old English meaning 'victorious town'. Short forms: Win, Winnie.

**Wolfgang:** From the Old German meaning 'path of the wolf' or 'travelling wolf'. Short forms: Wolf, Wolfie.

**Wyatt:** From the Old English meaning 'water'.

**Wyn:** From the Welsh meaning 'white', 'pure' or 'blessed'. Alternative spelling: Wynne.

## X

**Xander:** See Alexander.

**Xavier:** From the Arabic meaning 'splendid', 'bright' or the Basque meaning 'owner of a new house'. Alternative spellings: Javier, Zavier.

**Xerxes:** From the Persian meaning 'king'.

## Y

**Yehudi:** From the Hebrew meaning 'praise of the Lord'.

**Ynyr**: From the Welsh possibly meaning 'honour'.

**Yorick**: See George.

**Yuri**: See George.

**Yves**: See Ivo, Evan, John.

## Z

**Zachary**: From the Hebrew meaning 'God has remembered'. Alternative spellings: Sachairi, Zacary, Zacharius, Zachery, Zackary, Zackery. Short form: Zach, Zak.

**Zander**: See Alexander.

**Zane**: See John.

**Zavier**: See Xavier.

**Zebedee**: From the Hebrew meaning 'gift of God'. Alternative spelling: Zebediah. Short form: Zeb.

**Zedekiah**: From the Hebrew meaning 'God is righteousness' or 'God's justice'. Short form: Zed.

# Girls' Names

## A

**Aaryanna**: Combination of Aaron and Anna, possibly meaning 'holy beauty'.

**Abbrielle**: See Abigail.

**Abia**: From the Arabic meaning 'great'.

**Abigail**: From the Hebrew meaning 'father rejoices'. Alternative spellings: Abbrielle, Avigail. Short forms: Abbie, Abby, Gail.

**Abira**: From the Hebrew meaning 'my strength', 'strong' or 'heroic'. Alternative spellings: Adira, Amiza.

**Acacia**: From the Greek meaning 'immortality', 'resurrection'.

**Ada**: From the Old German meaning 'noble'. Alternative spellings: Addie, Aida, Eda, Edna.

**Adah**: From the Hebrew meaning 'beauty', 'ornament'.

**Adela**: From the Old German meaning 'noble'. Alternative spellings: Addeline, Adeline, Adella, Adelle, Adlina, Adline, Alina, Aline, Delaney, Edeline. Short form: Ada, Addi, Addie, Addy, Dela, Dele, Della, Lela.

**Adelaide**: From the Old German meaning 'noble sort'. Alternative spellings: Adalind, Adakube.

**Adin**: From the Old Norse meaning 'delicate' or the Hebrew meaning 'slender' or 'noble'. Alternative spelling: Adina.

**Adora:** From the Latin and French meaning 'worthy of divine worship'.

**Adriana:** The feminine form of Adrian (see Boys' Names). Alternative spellings: Adria, Adrianne.

**Adrienne:** From the Latin and Greek meaning 'rich', 'black' or 'mysterious'. Alternative spellings: Adrien, Adrina, Hardia.

**Afra:** From the Hebrew meaning 'young female deer'.

**Afton:** From the English village of this name.

**Agatha:** From the Greek meaning 'good', 'kind'. Alternative spellings: Agata, Aggie.

**Agnes:** From the Greek meaning 'pure', 'chaste'. Alternative spellings: Agnessa, Agnetis, Agnetta, Agnette, Aigneis, Annais, Anneyce, Anneys, Annice. Short forms: Aggi, Aggie, Agna, Agneti, Anice, Anise, Annice, Annis, Nesa, Nesi, Nessa, Nessi, Nessie, Nessy, Neta, Netta.

**Aida:** From the French or Latin meaning 'help'.

**Aileen:** See Helen. Alternative spellings: Ailene, Aleen, Alena, Eileen, Eilidh, Elene. Short forms: Aila, Lena.

**Ailie:** The Irish diminutive form of Helen.

**Ailsa:** From Scottish after Ailsa Craig, the rock in the Firth of Clyde, possibly meaning 'island dweller'.

**Aimee:** From the French meaning 'beloved'. Alternative spelling: Amy.

**Ainsley**: See Boys' Names.

**Aisha**: From the Arabic meaning 'prospering' or 'woman'. Alternative spellings: Aesha, Aiesha, Aishah, Aisia, Asha, Ahia, Ayeisha, Ayesha, Aysha, Ayshia.

**Aithne**: From the Celtic meaning 'little fire'.

**Alameda**: From the Spanish meaning 'poplar tree'.

**Alana**: From the Celtic meaning 'distant place' or 'fair', 'beautiful'. Short form: Lana.

**Alanis**: The feminine form of Alan (see Boys' Names).

**Alathea**: From the Greek meaning 'truth'. Alternative spelling: Aletta.

**Alberta**: The feminine form of Albert (see Boys' Names). Alternative spellings: Albertina, Albertine.

**Albine**: From the Latin meaning 'white'.

**Aleisha**: Possibly from the Arabic word *a'isha* meaning 'alive and well' or 'to live' or a form of Alicia. Alternative spelling: Alisha.

**Alethea**: From the Greek meaning 'truth'. Alternative spelling: Oletha.

**Alexandra**: The feminine form of Alexander (see Boys' Names). Alternative spellings: Alejandra, Alessandra. Short forms: Alex, Alexa. Olexa, Sacha, Sandra, Sandrine, Sasha.

**Alexis**: From the Greek meaning 'helper'.

**Alfreda**: The feminine form of Alfred (see Boys' Names). Alternative spellings: Alfredda, Alfreeda, Alfrieda, Elfrida.

Short form: Alfi, Alfie, Alfy.

**Alice:** From the Old German meaning 'nobility'. Alternative spellings: Alicia, Alison, Alissa, Alyssa, Alyssia, Allyce. Short forms: Ali, Allie, Ally.

**Alida:** From the Spanish meaning 'noble', 'kind' or the French meaning 'beautifully dressed'.

**Alina:** From the Arabic meaning 'noble' or 'illustrious'

**Alisa:** From the Ancient Aramaic meaning 'joy'. Alternative spelling: Aliza.

**Alison:** See Alice.

**Allegra:** From the Italian meaning 'jaunty', 'cheerful', 'lively'.

**Alma:** From the Hebrew meaning 'maiden' or the Latin meaning 'kind'.

**Almarina:** From the Latin meaning 'soul of the sea'.

**Alona:** From the Hebrew meaning 'oak tree'. Short form: Al, Ally, Loni.

**Althea:** From the Greek meaning 'healer'.

**Alyssa:** See Alice.

**Amabel:** From the Latin meaning 'loveable'. Alternative spellings: Anabel, Anabelle.

**Amaline:** See Amelia.

**Amalita:** See Amelia.

**Amanda:** From the Latin meaning 'worthy of love', 'loveable'. Short forms: Manda, Mandee, Mandi, Mandie, Mandy.

**Amerinda**: From the Greek meaning 'long-lived'.

**Amber**: From the Arabic meaning 'jewel'.

**Ambrosia**: From the Greek meaning 'elixir of love' or possibly from the Gothic *amala* meaning 'industrious'.

**Amelia**: From the Latin meaning 'toil', 'work'. Alternative spellings: Amaline, Amalita, Emelia, Emily. Short forms: Ami, Amie, Amy, Em, Melia, Milly.

**Ami**: Either from the English or African origins meaning 'beloved' or the French meaning 'friend'. Alternative spelling: Amy.

**Amina**: From the Arabic meaning 'sure', 'believable', 'right', 'trustworthy', 'reliable', 'dependable'. Alternative spelling: Aminah.

**Amira**: From the Hebrew meaning 'speech' or the Arabic meaning 'princess'.

**Amity**: From the Latin meaning 'love' or 'friendship'.

**Amoura**: From the French meaning 'love'.

**Amy**: From the French meaning 'beloved'; see also Amelia, Ami. Alternative spelling: Ami.

**Anabelle**: See Amabel. Alternative spelling: Anabella.

**Anael**: From the Breton French *an* meaning 'wind' and *ael* meaning 'angel'.

**Anäis**: From the Greek meaning 'fruitful' or the Hebrew meaning 'gracious'.

**Anaïs**: The Catalan Spanish version of Ana or Anne.

**Anastasia:** From the Greek meaning 'resurrection'. Short form: Nastasia, Stacey.

**Anchoret:** From the Welsh meaning 'much loved'.

**Andrea:** Possibly from the Greek meaning 'womanly' or the feminine form of Andreas (See Boys' Names). Alternative spelling: Andra, Adreana, Andreea, Andria, Andrienne, Andrietta, Adrina, Androulla, Ondrea. Short forms: Andie, Andre, Andrie, Andy, Dreena, Drena, Drina, Rena, Rina.

**Andromeda:** From the Greek meaning 'rescued'.

**Anemone:** From the Greek meaning 'wind flower'.

**Angela:** From the Greek meaning 'messenger'. Alternative spellings: Angelia, Angelina. Short forms: Angel, Angie.

**Angelica:** From the Latin *angelicus* meaning 'angelic' or the French meaning 'like an angel'. Short forms: Angel, Angie.

**Angharad:** From the Welsh meaning 'much loved'.

**Anika:** From the African meaning 'smart', 'beautiful' or 'child of god'.

**Anise:** See Agnes. Alternative spellings: Annice, Annis, Anissa, Annys. Short form: Ani.

**Anissa:** See Anise.

**Anita:** See Anne. Short form: Nita.

**Ann:** See Anne.

**Anna:** See Anne.

**Annabel:** See Amabel. Alternative spelling: Anabelle, Annabella.

**Anne**: From the Hebrew meaning 'grace' or 'favoured'. Alternative spellings: Anaïs, Ana, Anci, Andula, Andulka, Anette, Anicka, Ania, Anita, Ann, Anna, Annchen, Anneli, Anneke, Annette, Anni, Annie, Anny, Anouk, Anya, Hanna, Hannah, Hanne, Nan, Nana, Nani, Nancy, Nanna, Noula, Nina, Ninon, Nita.

**Anneke**: See Anne.

**Anneliese**: From the Latin meaning 'graced with God's bounty'.

**Annette**: See Anne. Short form: Anne, Annie, Netta, Nettie.

**Annunciata**: From the Latin meaning 'bearer of news'.

**Anouk**: See Anne.

**Anthea**: From the Greek *antheios* meaning 'flowery'.

**Antoinette**: See Antonia.

**Antonia**: The feminine form of Anthony (see Boys' Names). Alternative spelling: Antoineta, Antointetta, Antoinette, Antonie. Short forms: Anna, Ant, Nina, Netta, Netti, Toinetta, Toinette, Toni, Toni, Tonia, Toney, Tony.

**Anwen**: From the Welsh meaning 'very beautiful'.

**Anya**: See Anne.

**Aoife**: From the Gaelic meaning 'radiant'. Alternative spelling: Eve.

**Aphra**: From the Hebrew meaning 'young doe'.

**April**: From the Latin meaning 'opening'. Alternative spelling: Avril.

**Arabella:** From the Latin meaning 'beautiful altar' or the German meaning 'eagle'. Short forms: Bel, Bella.

**Araminta:** Meaning unknown. Short forms: Minta, Minty.

**Ariadne:** From the Greek meaning 'very divine','holy'.

**Arianna:** From the Welsh *arian* meaning 'silver'. Alternative spelling: Ariana.

**Arianne:** From the Greek meaning 'the very holy' or 'pleasing one'. Alternative spellings: Ariane.

**Arienwen:** From the Welsh meaning 'silver'.

**Ariel:** From the Hebrew meaning 'lion of God'. Alternative spellings: Arielle, Ariela. Short form: Ari.

**Arienhwyfar:** From the Welsh meaning 'snowy owl' implying a fair and wise disposition.

**Aris:** Possibly from the Greek name Aristides meaning 'best' or 'excellent'.

**Arleen:** From the Irish meaning 'pledge'. Alternative spelling: Arlene.

**Armeria:** From the Latin *flos armeriae*, a species of the flower dianthus.

**Arwenna:** From the Welsh meaning 'muse'.

**Asa:** From the Japanese meaning 'born in the morning' or the Hebrew meaning 'doctor', 'healer'.

**Asha:** Feminine variation of Asher or Ashleigh (See Boys' Names).

**Ashleigh:** See Boys' Names. Alternative spellings: Ashley, Ashlyn.

**Astra:** From the Greek meaning 'star'.

**Astrid:** From the Scandinavian *áss* meaning 'god' and *frior* meaning 'fair' or possibly the Old Norse meaning 'divine strength'.

**Atalanta:** From the Greek meaning 'mighty huntress'.

**Athena:** From the Greek meaning 'wise'.

**Aubrianna:** Combination of the names Aubrey (see Boys' Names) and Brianna.

**Audrey:** From the Old English name Ethelreda meaning 'strength'. Aleternative spellings: Audey, Audi, Audree, Audri, Audrie, Audry.

**Augusta:** From the Latin meaning 'venerable'.

**Aurelia:** From the Latin meaning 'golden'. Alternative spelling: Oralia.

**Aurora:** From the Latin meaning 'dawn'.

**Ava:** From the Latin meaning 'bird'.

**Avis:** From the Old German meaning 'refuge in war' or the Latin meaning 'bird'. Short form: Ava.

**Avril:** See April.

**Ayesha:** See Aisha.

## B

**Bailey:** See Boys' Names. Alternative spelling: Bayleigh.

**Bambi:** From the Italian meaning 'little child'.

**Barbera:** From the Latin meaning 'foreign' or 'stranger'.

Alternative spelling: Barbara. Short forms: Babs, Barb.

**Bathsheba:** From the Hebrew meaning 'daughter of opulence' or 'daughter of an oath'. Alternative spelling: Batsheba. Short form: Sheba.

**Batya:** From the Hebrew meaning 'daughter of God'.

**Beatrice:** The Italian and French form of Beatrix.

**Beatrix:** From the Latin meaning 'bringer of happiness'. Alternative spellings: Beatriks, Beatrise, Beitiris, Betrys. Short forms: Bee, Bea, Trixie, Trixy.

**Becky:** See Rebecca.

**Behira:** From the Arabic meaning 'dazzling'.

**Belinda:** From the Old English meaning 'very beautiful' or the Old Spanish meaning 'pretty'.

**Bella:** From the Latin meaning 'fair', 'lovely one'; see also Arabella or Isabella. Alternative spelling: Belle.

**Benita:** From the Latin meaning 'blessed'.

**Bernadette:** The feminine form of Bernard (See Boys' Names).

**Bernice:** From the Greek meaning 'bringer of victory'. Alternative spelling: Berenice.

**Bertha:** From the Old German meaning 'bright'. Alternative spelling: Bertina.

**Beryl:** From the Greek meaning 'sea-green jewel'; the Sanskrit meaning 'precious stone' or the Arabic meaning 'crystal' or 'very clear'.

**Bess:** See Elizabeth.

**Beth:** From the Hebrew meaning 'house'; see also Elizabeth.

**Bethan:** See Elizabeth.

**Bethag:** From the Gaelic meaning 'life'.

**Bethany:** Possibly from the Hebrew *beth te' ena* meaning 'house of figs' or the Aramaic meaning 'house of poverty'.

**Betsy:** See Elizabeth.

**Betty:** See Elizabeth.

**Beulah:** From the Hebrew meaning 'claimed as wife' or 'she who is to be married/ruled over'.

**Beverly:** From the Old English meaning 'beaver meadow'.

**Bevin:** From the Irish Gaelic meaning 'sweet-singing maiden'. Alternative spelling: Béibhinn.

**Bianca:** From the Italian meaning 'white' or 'pure'. Alternative spelling: Blanche.

**Bibi:** From the French meaning 'toy', 'bauble' or the Arabic meaning 'lady'.

**Bijou:** From the French meaning 'jewel'.

**Billie:** A short form of Wilelmina.

**Bina:** From the Hebrew meaning 'wise', 'understanding'.

**Binnie:** From the Celtic meaning 'crib', 'wicker basket'.

**Birgitta:** From the Scandinavian meaning 'strong'.

**Blair:** From the Scottish Gaelic meaning 'from the flat/level place'.

**Blake:** From the English meaning 'black'.

**Blanche:** From the French meaning 'white'. Alternative spellings: Bianca, Branka, Blanca.

**Bliss:** From the Old English meaning 'happiness', 'joy'.

**Blodwedd:** From the Welsh meaning 'flower face'.

**Blodwen:** From the Welsh meaning 'white flower'.

**Blossom:** From the Old English meaning 'a plant or tree in flower'.

**Blythe:** From the English *blithe* meaning 'happy' or 'cheerful'.

**Bo:** From the Chinese meaning 'precious' or the Old Norse meaning 'householder'.

**Bobbie:** See Roberta.

**Bonita:** From the Spanish meaning 'little good one' or 'pretty'.

**Bonnie:** From the Latin meaning 'good'.

**Brandy:** Possibly a feminine form of the name Brandon (see Boys' Names); from the Old English meaning 'to burn wine'; from the fortified wine or from the Italian surname Brand meaning 'sword'. Alternative spelling: Brandi.

**Branwen:** From the Welsh meaning 'white raven', 'holy raven'. Alternative spelling: Bronwen.

**Breda:** See Bridget.

**Bree:** From the Middle English meaning 'broth' or the Irish meaning 'hill'.

**Breeya:** From the Gaelic *brigh* meaning 'strength' or 'force'.

**Brenda:** The feminine form of Brendan (See Boys' Names) or from the Scandinavian *brand* meaning 'burning sword' or the Irish meaning 'princess'. Alternative spelling: Brenna.

**Brenna**: See Brenda.

**Brett**: See Boys' Names.

**Briana**: Feminine form of Brian (see Boys' Names). Alternative spellings: Breanna, Breanne, Brianna, Brianne, Brina, Bryana, Bryanna, Bryanne.

**Brice**: See Boys' Names. Alternative spelling: Bryce.

**Bridget**: From the Celtic meaning 'strength' or 'high'. Alternative spelling: Breda.

**Brigette**: From the Irish meaning 'bold' or 'strong'. Alternative spellings: Brigit, Bridgeda.

**Briony**: From the Greek *bryonia* meaning 'climbing vine'. Alternative spelling: Bryony. Short form: Bry.

**Britt**: From the Scandinavian meaning 'strength'.

**Brittney**: From the Latin meaning 'from Britain'.

**Britta**: From the Old English meaning 'pride'.

**Bronte**: From the Greek meaning 'thunder'.

**Bronwen**: From the Welsh meaning 'white breast'. Alternative spelling: Bronwyn.

**Brooke**: From the Old English *broc* meaning 'water', 'stream'.

**Brooklyn**: From the area of New York City.

**Brunhild**: From the Old High German meaning 'someone well-prepared for life's struggle' or 'armoured warrior'. Alternative spelling: Brunhilda.

**Bryce:** See Brice.

**Bryn:** From the Welsh meaning 'hill' or 'mountain'.

**Bryna:** From the Irish Gaelic meaning 'strength'.

**Buffy:** From the American buffalo meaning 'from the plains' or a pet form of Elizabeth.

**Bunty:** Possibly from the English 'bunny' meaning 'little rabbit'.

## C

**Cailin:** See Colleen.

**Caitlin:** The Gaelic form of Catherine. Alternative spellings: Katelyn, Caitlyn.

**Callie:** See Caroline.

**Calliope:** From the Greek meaning 'beautiful voice'.

**Callista:** From the Greek meaning 'most beautiful'. Alternative spelling: Calista.

**Calpurnia:** From the Greek meaning 'beautiful prostitute'.

**Calypso:** From the Greek meaning 'concealer' or 'to conceal'.

**Camelia:** See Camilla.

**Cameo:** From the Italian meaning 'jewel'.

**Cameron:** From the Scottish meaning 'crooked nose'. Alternative spelling: Kameron. Short forms: Cam, Cammie.

**Camilla:** From the Latin meaning 'attendant at a sacrifice/ceremony'. Alternative spellings: Camelia, Camille. Short form: Cam, Cami, Cammi, Cammie, Cammy, Milla,

Milli, Millie, Milly, Kamilla.

**Camille**: See Camilla.

**Candace**: From the Greek meaning 'glittering white', 'glowing'. Alternative spellings: Candice, Candida. Short form: Candy.

**Candice**: See Candace.

**Candida**: See Candace.

**Candy**: See Candace.

**Caprice**: From the French meaning 'whimisical', 'unpredictable' or the Italian meaning 'fanciful'.

**Cara**: From the Gaelic meaning 'friend' or the Latin meaning 'dear'. Alternative spellings: Careen, Carey.

**Caresse**: From the French meaning 'tender touch'.

**Careen**: See Cara.

**Carey**: See Cara or Caroline. Alternative spelling: Carrie.

**Caridad**: From the Spanish meaning 'charity'.

**Carina**: From the Italian meaning 'dear little one'. Short form: Rina.

**Carissa**: From the Latin meaning 'dear one'. Alternative spellings: Caressa, Carice, Carisa, Karessa, Karisa, Karise. Short forms: Cari, Carie.

**Carita**: From the Latin meaning 'kindness'.

**Carla**: From the Old German meaning 'free woman'. Alternative spellings: Carleia, Carlene, Carley, Carlie, Carly, Karly.

**Carleia**: See Carla.

**Carlene**: See Carla.

**Carlin**: See Caroline.

**Carlotta**: See Charlotte. Short form: Lola.

**Carly**: See Carla.

**Carmel**: From the Hebrew meaning 'the garden'.

**Carmela**: From the Latin meaning 'fruitful orchard'. Alternative spelling: Carmella.

**Carmen**: From the Latin meaning 'song'. Alternative spelling: Charmaine.

**Carol**: From the Old French meaning 'to celebrate in song' or the possibly the Latin meaing 'strong and womanly'; see also Caroline.

**Carolina**: See Caroline.

**Caroline**: A feminine form of Charles (See Boys' Names). Alternative spellings: Carlin, Carolina, Carolyn, Carolyne, Karoline. Short forms: Callie, Carrie, Carol, Carrie, Karrie, Lynne.

**Carrie**: See Caroline.

**Caryn**: See Karen.

**Caryon**: See Catherine.

**Carys**: From the Welsh meaning 'love' or possibly 'helper of men'. Alternative spellings: Caris, Ceri, Cerise, Cerys.

**Cassandra**: From the Greek meaning 'the confuser of men'. Alternative spellings: Kassandra. Short forms: Cass, Cassie, Cassy, Sandi, Sandra.

**Cassia:** From the Greek meaning 'herb'.

**Cassidy:** From the Irish meaning 'curly-headed' or 'clever'. Alternative spelling: Kassady. Short forms: Cass, Cassie.

**Cassie:** See Cassandra.

**Catalina:** The Spanish derivative of Catherine.

**Cate:** See Catherine.

**Catherine:** From the Greek *katharos* meaning 'pure'. Alternative spellings: Caitlin, Caryon, Catalina, Cathleen, Cathryn, Catriona, Kaitlin, Katalina, Katarina, Katena, Katerina, Katharin, Katharine, Katherine, Kathleen, Kathrin, Kathrine, Kathryn, Kathryne, Kathrynn, Katria, Katriana, Katriane, Katrina, Katrine, Katina, Katrya. Short forms: Cate, Catrina, Kara, Karen, Karesa, Karina, Kate, Katie, Kitty, Kathy, Kathie.

**Cathleen:** See Catherine.

**Catrina:** See Catherine.

**Catriona:** See Catherine.

**Cayla:** See Kay.

**Cecilia:** The feminine form of Cecil (see Boys' Names). Alternative spellings: Cecile, Cicely, Cissy, Sisley.

**Cedra:** Possibly the feminine version of Cedric (see Boys' Names).

**Celene:** From the Latin meaning 'heaven' or the Greek meaning 'moon'. Alternative spellings: Celina, Céline, Salena, Selene, Selina, Sheila.

**Celeste:** From the Latin meaning 'heavenly'. Alternative spellings:

Celesta, Celestin, Celestina, Celestine. Short forms: Celia, Tyna, Cela, Celie, Cesia.

**Celia**: From the Latin *caelum* meaning 'heaven'; see also Celeste.

**Ceres**: From the Latin meaning 'of the spring'.

**Ceri**: See Carys.

**Cerise**: From the French meaning 'cherry'.

**Cerys**: See Carys.

**Chandra**: From the Hindu god of the moon or the Sanskrit meaning 'moon'.

**Chanel**: Possibly from the Old French *chandele* meaning 'candle maker'; also after Coco Chanel.

**Chantal**: From the French meaning 'singer'. Alternative spelling: Chantelle.

**Charis**: From the Greek meaning 'grace', 'kindness'.

**Charity**: From the Latin meaning 'benevolent goodwill and hope' or the Latin *caritas* meaning 'caring for and loving others'.

**Charlene**: A feminine form of Charles (see Boys' Names). Alternative spelling: Sharlene.

**Charlotte**: From the Old German meaning 'free woman' or 'small woman'. Alternative spellings: Carla, Carlotta, Charlene, Charlet, Charletta, Charlette, Charline, Charlott, Charlotta, Charlotty, Charmaine, Charolet, Charolette. Short forms: Carly, Char, Chara, Charl, Charla, Charle, Charlie, Charlisa, Charlita, Charlo, Lots, Lotte, Lottie, Lotty.

**Charmaine**: From the Roman clan name Carmineus ; the Greek meaning 'mother of joy' or possibly the Latin meaning 'a singer'; see also Carmen. Alternative spelling: Charmain.

**Chastity**: From the Latin meaning 'purity', 'innocence'.

**Chaya:** From the Hebrew meaning 'life'.

**Chelsea**: From the Old English meaning 'ship's port' or possibly from the area of London. Alternative spelling: Chelsie.

**Cher**: From the French meaning 'beloved'.

**Cheri**: From the French *chérie* meaning 'dear or love'. Alternative spellings: Charlene, Cherie, Cheryl.

**Cherish**: From the English meaning 'dearly beloved'.

**Cherry**: From the fruit.

**Cheryl**: Possibly from the French *chérie* meaning 'dear'. Alternative spelling: Sheryl.

**Chesna**: From the Slavic meaning 'peaceful'.

**Chessa**: From the Slavic meaning 'at peace'.

**Chiara**: The Italian form of Clare. Alternative spelling: Kira.

**Chloe**: From the Greek meaning 'a green shoot', 'fresh blooming', 'verdant'.

**Chloris**: From the Greek meaning 'pale'.

**Chris**: See Christina.

**Christa**: See Christina.

**Christie**: See Christina.

**Christina**: From the Greek or Latin meaning 'christian'. Alternative spellings: Christabel, Christel, Christen, Christine, Kirsten, Kirstin, Kristen, Kristina. Short forms: Chris, Chrissy, Christa, Christie, Crista, Christy, Kirsty, Kris, Krista, Kristi, Kristie, Kristy, Ina, Tina.

**Christine**: See Christina.

**Christy**: See Christina.

**Chrysanthe**: From the Greek meaning 'precious flower'. Alternative spelling: Chrysantha.

**Ciara**: The Irish feminine form of Ciaran (see Boys' Names). Alternative spellings: Ciar, Kara, Kiara, Kiera.

**Cicely**: See Cecelia.

**Cilla**: See Priscilla.

**Cindy**: See Cynthia or Lucinda.

**Cira**: A feminine form of Cyril (see Boys' Names). Alternative spelling: Kira.

**Cissy**: See Cecilia.

**Clara**: From the Latin meaning 'clear', 'bright'.

**Clare**: From the Latin meaning 'famous'. Alternative spellings: Chiara, Clair, Claire, Clairine, Clarina, Clarine, Clarita, Clarissa.

**Claribel**: From the English meaning 'bright', 'beautiful'. Alternative spelling: Clarabelle.

**Clarice**: See Clarissa. Alternative spelling: Clarise.

**Clarissa**: From the Greek meaning 'brilliant'; see also Clare. Alternative spelling: Klarissa. Short forms: Clarice, Clarise.

**Claudette**: See Claudia.

**Claudia**: From the Latin meaning 'lame'. Alternative spellings: Claudette, Claudine. Short forms: Claudi, Claudie, Claude.

**Clea**: See Cleo.

**Clemency**: From the Latin meaning 'mildness'.

**Clementine**: From the Latin meaning 'merciful'.

**Cleo**: From the Greek meaning 'glory'; see also Cleopatra. Alternative spelling: Clea.

**Cleopatra**: From the Greek meaning 'glory of her father'. Short form: Cleo.

**Clio**: From the Greek meaning 'proclaimer', 'glorifier'.

**Clotilda**: From the German meaning 'heroine' or the Old German meaning 'loud battle'.

**Cody**: From the Irish meaning 'helpful'. Alternative spellings: Codey, Codi, Codie, Kodey, Kodi, Kodie, Kody.

**Coleen**: From the Irish meaning 'girl'. Alternative spellings: Colleen, Cailin.

**Colette**: The feminine form of Colin (See Boys' Names); see also Nichole. Alternative spellings: Collette.

**Colleen**: From the Irish meaning 'girl'. Alternative spellings: Colene, Coline, Collen, Collene, Colline.

**Connie**: See Constance.

**Constance**: From the Latin meaning 'faithful'. Alternative spellings: Constancia, Constanta, Constantia, Constanz, Konstance,

Konstantin, Konstanze. Short form: Con, Conni, Connie, Conny.

**Consuelo**: From the Latin meaning 'consolation'.

**Cora**: Possibly from the Greek *kore* meaning 'maiden'. Alternative spellings: Coretta, Corey, Cory, Kora.

**Coral**: From the Latin meaning 'from the sea'.

**Cordelia**: From the Latin meaning 'warm-hearted', 'good-hearted'; the Welsh meaning 'sea jewel' or the Celtic meaning 'daughter of the sea'.

**Corentine**: See Corinne.

**Coretta**: See Cora.

**Corinna**: From the Greek *korinna* meaning 'maiden'. Alternative spellings: Corentine, Corina, Corinne. Short forms: Cri, Corey, Cory, Kore.

**Cornelia**: Feminine form of Cornelius (see Boys' Names).

**Cory**: See Cora. Alternative spelling: Corey.

**Cosima**: From the Greek meaning 'universe', 'harmony'.

**Courtney**: Possibly from the Old English meaning 'court dweller', 'from the court' or the English meaning 'courteous'.

**Cressida**: From the Greek meaning 'golden one'.

**Crista**: See Christina.

**Crystal**: From the French meaning 'clear' or 'brilliant'. Alternative spellings: Cristel, Krystal.

**Cybil**: From the Greek meaning 'prophet'. Alternative spellings: Cybele, Sibyl, Sybyl.

**Cydney:** See Sydney.

**Cynthia:** From Kynthia the Greek goddess of wild animals or from the Greek meaning 'moon'; see also Hyacinth or Sancha. Alternative spellings: Cynthiana, Cynthie, Hyacinth, Kynthia. Short forms: Cinda, Cindee, Cindi, Cindie, Cindy, Cyndie, Cyndy, Cynth, Kynthia, Sindee, Sindy, Tia.

**Cyrilla:** From the Greek meaning 'mistress', 'lady'.

## D

**Daffodile:** From the Greek *asphodelos* meaning 'bright yellow spring flower'. Alternative spelling: Daffodil.

**Dagmar:** From the Danish meaning 'joy of the Dane' or 'glorious'.

**Dahlia:** From the Scandinavian meaning 'valley' or the flower.

**Daisy:** From the Old English meaning 'day's eye' or the flower. Alternative spellings: Daisia, Daisie, Dasey, Dasi, Dasie, Daysee, Daysie, Daysy.

**Dale:** From the Old English meaning 'valley'.

**Dalia:** From the Arabic meaning 'gentle'.

**Damalis:** From the Greek meaning 'tamer', 'conqueror'.

**Damaris:** From the Greek meaning 'heifer' or 'calf' implying gentleness or the Latin meaning 'gentle'.

**Dana:** From the Celtic 'Queen of the Danes' or 'from Denmark'; see also Daniella. Alternative spellings: Daina, Dane, Danna, Dansy, Dayna.

**Daniele**: See Daniella. Alternative spelling: Danielle.

**Daniella**: From the Hebrew meaning 'God has judged'. Alternative spellings: Daniele, Danielle. Short form: Dana.

**Danita**: Possibly from the Latin meaning 'given by God'. Alternative spellings: Danicka, Danuta.

**Daphne**: From the Greek meaning 'laurel bush' or 'bay tree'. Alternative spellings: Daphna, Daphnee.

**Dara**: From the Middle English meaning 'compassion', 'to have courage' or 'daring' or possibly from the Hebrew meaning 'pearl of wisdom'.

**Darby**: From the English meaning 'deer park'.

**Darcy**: From the Irish meaning 'dark' or the French meaning 'fortress' or' from the fortress'. Alternative spellings: Darcey, Darci, Darcie.

**Daria**: The feminine form of Darius.

**Darleen**: From the Old English *deorling* meaning 'beloved', 'worthy' or 'favourite'. Alternative spelling: Darlene.

**Daryn**: From the Greek meaning 'gift'. Alternative spelling: Darin.

**Davan**: The Gaelic feminine form of David (see Boys' Names). Alternative spelling: Davene.

**Davene**: See Davan.

**Davina**: From the Hebrew meaning 'beloved'.

**Dawn**: From the English meaning 'daybreak'.

**Deanna**: From the Latin meaning 'bright as day'. or the Old

English meaning 'from the valley'.

**Deborah:** From the Hebrew meaning 'wisdom'. Alternative spellings: Debora, Decora, Devera, Devorah, Devrah. Short forms: Deb, Debbi, Debbie, Debo, Debra. Dedra, Deidra, Deidre.

**Decima:** The feminine form of Decimus (see Boys' Names).

**Dee:** From the Welsh meaning 'black', 'dark'.

**Deirdre:** From the Celtic meaning 'one who rages'; the Gaelic meaning 'broken-hearted' or the Middle English meaning 'young girl'. Alternative spellings: Deidra, Dedra, Deidrie, Diedre.

**Dela:** See Adela.

**Delaney:** From the Irish meaning 'defender of the challenger'; see also Adela.

**Delicia:** From the Latin meaning 'to give pleasure', 'to charm'.

**Delilah:** From the Arabic meaning 'guide', 'leader' or the Hebrew meaning 'poor' or 'hair'.

**Delma:** From the Spanish meaning 'of the sea' or possibly the German meaning 'noble protector'. Alternative spelling: Delmar.

**Delpha:** From the Greek meaning 'dolphin'. Alternative spellings: Delphine, Delfine.

**Demetria:** The feminine form of Demetrius (see Boys' Names). Short form: Demi.

**Demi:** From the French meaning 'half'; see also Demetria

**Dena:** From the Anglo-Saxon meaning 'glen'. Alternative spelling:

Denna.

**Denise:** The feminine form of Denis (see Boys' Names).

**Dervla:** From the Irish meaning 'daughter of the poet'.

**Desdemona:** From the Greek meaning 'woman of bad fortune'.

**Desirée:** From the Old French meaning 'hope' or 'desired'. Alternative spelling: Desire.

**Desma:** From the Greek meaning 'bond', 'pledge'.

**Desta:** From the French 'destiny'.

**Deva:** From the Sanskrit meaning 'god', 'divine'.

**Devi:** From the Hindi meaning 'goddess'.

**Devon:** See Boys' Names.

**Dextra:** From the Latin meaning 'right-hand side'.

**Diamanta:** From the Greek meaning 'unconquerable'.

**Diana:** From the Latin dius meaning 'god-like', 'divine'. Alternative spellings: Dianna, Dianne, Deana, Deanna, Dyann. Short forms: Dee, Di, Dian.

**Dilys:** From the Welsh meaning 'genuine', 'perfect', 'true'.

**Dinah:** From the Hebrew meaning 'vindication' or 'judgement'.

**Dione:** From the Greek meaning 'divine queen'. Alternative spelling: Dion, Dionis, Dionne.

**Dionisia:** A feminine form of Dionysis (see Boys' Names).

**Dionne:** See Dione.

**Dita:** See Edith.

**Diva:** From the Latin meaning 'goddess'.

**Divina**: From the Latin meaning 'divine one'.

**Dixie**: From the Old Norse meaning 'active spirit'.

**Dolores**: From the Spanish meaning 'grief', 'lady of sorrows'. Alternative spelling: Lolita. Short form: Dela, Dol, Lola.

**Dominica**: From the Latin meaning 'born on the Sabbath'. Short forms: Dom, Doma, Domin, Dominiee, Nica, Nika.

**Dominique**: From the Latin meaning 'belonging to God'. Alternative spellings: Dominica, Dominick, Dominik, Dominika. Short forms: Dom, Doma, Domin, Dominiee, Nica, Nika.

**Donalda**: The feminine form of Donald (see Boys' Names). Alternative spellings: Donella, Donelle, Donnelle.

**Donata**: From the Latin meaning 'gift' or 'deserving of gifts'.

**Donella**: See Donalda. Alternative spelling: Donnelle.

**Donna**: From the Italian meaning 'lady'.

**Dora**: See Dorothea.

**Doreen**: See Dorothea.

**Dorian**: Possibly from the Greek meaing 'child of the sea'.

**Doris**: From the Greek meaning 'bountiful', 'from the ocean' or 'sacrificial knife'.

**Dorit**: From the Hebrew *dor* meaning 'generation'. Alternative spelling: Doritt, Dorrit.

**Dorothea**: From the Greek meaning 'gift of God', 'divine gift'. Alternative spellings: Doraleen, Doreen, Dorene, Dorita, Dorothy, Dorrie, Dortha, Dorthy, Dory, Drinda. Short forms:

Dodi, Dodo, Dollie, Dolly, Dora, Dorat, Dori, Dory, Dot, Dotti, Dottie, Dotty, Thea.

**Drew**: A feminine form of Andrew (see Boys' Names).

**Druella**: From the Old German meaning 'elfin vision'.

**Drusilla**: From the Greek meaning 'soft-eyed' or the Latin meaning 'firm' or 'the strong one'. Alternative spelling: Drucie. Short forms: Dru, Druci.

**Dryden**: From the Old English meaning 'dry valley' or 'dry land'.

**Dulcie**: From the Latin meaning 'sweet'.

**Dusty**: The feminine form of Dustin (see Boys' Names).

## E

**Ea**: From the Greek, possibly the name of or meaning 'a goddess'.

**Eartha**: Possibly from the Old English meaning 'child of the earth'.

**Ebony**: From the Latin or Greek meaning 'dark', 'black'. Alternative spellings: Eboni, Ebonie.

**Edith**: From the Old English *ead* meaning 'wealthy' or 'fortunate' and *gyo* meaning 'war'. Alternative spellings: Edine, Editha, Edithe, Eidita. Short forms: Eade, Eda, Edda, Edie, Edy, Dita.

**Edna**: From the Hebrew meaning 'pleasure'; see also Ada.

**Edwina**: The feminine form of Edwin (see Boys' Names).

**Eileen**: See Helen. Alternative spellings: Aileen, Eilean, Eileen, Eilene, Ilene.

**Eilidh**: The Gaelic form of Aileen.

**Eiligh**: Gaelic form of Helen.

**Eira**: From the Welsh meaning 'snow'.

**Eireen**: See Irene.

**Eithne**: See Ethna.

**Eirlys**: From the Welsh meaning 'snowdrop'.

**Elaine**: From the Italian name Elettre, which comes from the Greek *elektor* meaning 'brilliant'; see also Helen. Alternative spellings: Elayne, Elana.

**Eleanor**: See Helen. Alternative spellings: Eleanour, Elana, Elanor, Eleanora, Eleanore, Elena, Elenore, Elinor, Elinore, Ellinore, Elnore, Elynor, Elynore, Nell, Noreen, Leonora, Leonore. Short form: Ellie, Nel, Nora.

**Elen**: From the Welsh meaning 'nymph'; see also Helen. Alternative spellings: Elin, Elan, Ellen, Nel.

**Elena**: See Helen.

**Elfrida**: Possibly the feminine form of Alfred (see Boys' Names). Short form: Frida.

**Elin**: See Elen.

**Elisa**: See Elizabeth.

**Elise**: See Elizabeth.

**Elizabeth**: From the Hebrew meaning 'oath of God'. Alternative spellings: Elisabet, Elisabeth, Elisveta. Short forms: Bet, Beta, Beth, Bethan, Betka, Betsi, Betsy, Bett, Betta, Bette, Bettina, Betty, Betuska, Bess, Bessi, Bessie, Bessy, Buffy, Ela, Elsa,

Elsbeth, Elisa, Elise, Elissa, Eliza, Ellie, Elsa, Else, Elsi, Elsie, Elspeth, Eylse, Eylssa, Illse, Isa, Isabella, Isabelle, Libbi, Libbie, Libby, Liese, Liesel, Lisa, Lisbet, Lisbeth, Lise, Lisette, Liz, Liza, Lizbeth, Lizabeth, Lizette, Lizzi, Lizzie, Lizzy.

**Ella**: From the Old German meaning 'all' or the English meaning 'elfin' or 'beautiful fairy woman'. Short form: Ellie.

**Ellen**: See Elen or Helen.

**Ellie**: Short form of Ella, Elizabeth, Eleanor or Elen. Alternative spelling: Elly.

**Elsa**: See Elizabeth.

**Elspeth**: See Elizabeth.

**Eluned**: From the Welsh meaning 'icon'.

**Elvira**: From the German *ali* meaning 'other' and *wer* meaning 'true'; the Latin meaning 'white' or 'blonde'; the Spanish meaning 'elfin'; the German meaning 'closed up' or the Old German *alverat* meaning 'wise counsel'.

**Emilia**: See Amelia, Emily.

**Emily**: From the Latin meaning 'flatterer'; the German meaning 'industrious' or the Roman clan name Aemilius. Alternative spellings: Em, Ema, Emaily, Emeli, Emeline, Emilee, Emili, Emilia, Emilienne, Emmalee, Emmalou, Emma, Emmie. See also Amelia.

**Emma**: From the German meaning 'universal', 'whole' or 'complete'; see also Emily.

**Enfys**: From the Welsh meaning 'rainbow'.

**Enid**: From the Welsh meaning 'lark', 'life' or 'spirit'.

**Epiphany**: From the Greek meaning 'to be enlightened'.

**Erica**: The feminine version of Eric (see Boys' Names). Alternative spellings: Erika.

**Erin**: From the Irish meaning 'Ireland' or the Old Norse meaning 'peace'.

**Ermintrude**: From the Old German *ermin* meaning 'whole' or 'universe' and *drudi* meaning 'strength'.

**Erna**: From the German form of Ernesta.

**Ernesta**: The feminine form of Ernest (see Boys' Names). Alternative spelling: Ernestine. Short form: Erna.

**Esmé**: From the French meaning 'esteemed'; see also Esmeralda.

**Esmeralda**: From the Spanish meaning 'emerald'. Alternative spelling: Esmerelda. Short form: Esmé.

**Estelle**: From the French meaning 'star'. Alternative spelling: Estella. Short form: Stella, Stelle.

**Esther**: From the Hebrew *hadassah* meaning 'myrtle' or the Persian *esthar* meaning 'evening star'. Alternative spellngs: Ester, Hester, Hetty. Short forms: Essa, Essi, Essy, Esta, Etti, Ettie, Etty.

**Ethel**: From the Old German or English meaning 'noble'.

**Ethna**: From the Irish meaning 'little fire'. Alternative spelling: Eithne.

**Eugenia**: From the Greek meaning 'excellent', 'well-born', 'fortunate'.

**Eunice**: From the Greek meaning 'happy', 'good' or 'victory'.

**Eurydice**: From the Greek meaning 'justice' or 'wide', 'broad'.

**Eva**: See Eve.

**Evangeline**: From the Greek meaning 'one who proclaims the gospel' or 'good news'. Alternative spelling: Evangelina. Short forms: Eve, Eva.

**Eve**: From the Hebrew *chavah* meaning 'life-giving' or 'life'. Alternative spellings: Aoiffe, Chava, Eba, Ebba, Eva, Evelin, Evelina, Evelyn, Evi, Evia, Evicka, Evin, Evita, Evka, Evlun, Ewa, Ina, Lina.

**Evelyn**: From the English, Old German or French meaning 'hazelnut'; see also Eve. Alternative spellings: Aveline, Evaline, Evelynne, Evline, Evlyne.

**Evette**: See Yvette.

**Evita**: See Eve.

## F

**Faith**: From the Latin meaning 'trust' or 'devotion'.

**Fallon**: From the Irish surname meaning 'leader' or 'grandchild of the ruler'.

**Fanny**: A feminine form for Francis (see Boys' Names); see also Frances.

**Farah**: From the Arabic meaning 'joy' or 'cheerfulness'.

**Farrah**: From the Middle English meaning 'beautiful' or 'pleasant' or the Arabic meaning 'happiness'.

**Fatima**: From the Arabic meaning 'gentle' or 'chaste'.

**Fawn**: From the French meaning 'young deer'.

**Fay**: From the French meaning 'fairy'. Alternative spellings: Fae, Faye.

**Felicia**: From the Latin meaning 'lucky'. Alternative spelling: Phylicia.

**Felicity**: From the Latin meaning 'happiness'.

**Fenella**: From the Gaelic meaning 'white shoulder'. Alternative spellings: Finella, Finola, Finnoula, Fionnuala, Fionnula.Short form: Nola, Nuala.

**Feodorea**: The feminine form of Theodore (see Boys' Names). Fedora, Fedoria.

**Fern**: From the plant.

**Ffion**: From the Welsh meaning 'foxglove flower'.

**Fifi**: See Josephine.

**Finola**: See Fenella.

**Fiona**: From the Gaelic meaning 'fair' or 'white'. Short form: Fi.

**Fleur**: From the French meaning 'flower'.

**Flora**: From the Latin meaning 'flower'. Short forms: Flo, Florry.

**Florence**: From the Latin meaning 'blooming' or 'flourishing'. Short forms: Florry, Florrie, Flo.

**Frances**: From the Latin meaning 'Frenchwoman' or possibly 'free woman'. Alternative spellings: Françoise, Francine, Paquita. Short forms: Fanny, Frankie, Frannie, Franny.

**Francesca:** From the Italian meaning 'French'.

**Frederica:** The feminine form of Frederick (see Boys' Names). Alternative spelling: Frederique. Short forms: Freda, Freddie, Frida, Frieda, Fryda.

**Freda:** See Elfrida, Frederica or Winifred.

**Freya:** From the Norse meaning 'noble lady'. Alternative spellings: Freja, Freyja, Froja.

**Frieda:** From the Old German meaning 'peace'. Alternative spellings: Freda, Frida.

## G

**Gabrielle:** From the Hebrew meaning 'strong woman of God' or possibly 'God is my strength'. Alternative spellings: Gabriela, Gabriella. Short form: Gabby, Gabbie, Gabi, Gaby, Gay.

**Gaia:** From the Greek *gé* meaning 'earth'. Alternative spelling: Gaea.

**Gail:** See Abigail.

**Gaynor:** See Guinevere.

**Gemma:** From the Italian meaning 'gem' or 'precious stone'. Alternative spellings: Jemma, Germaine.

**Genevieve:** From the German meaning 'fair one' or the Welsh meaning 'fair', 'white-browed' or 'white wave'. Alternative spellings: Gaynor, Guenevere, Guenivere,

Gwendolyn, Jennifer. Short forms: Gena, Genna, Gina, Gennie, Genny, Jenni, Jennie, Jenny.

**Georgeanne**: See Georgiana.

**Georgia**: See Georgina.

**Georgiana**: See Georgina.

**Georgina**: The feminine form of George (See Boys' Names). Alternative spellings: Georgeanne, Georgette, Georgia, Georgiana, Georgina, Georgine. Short forms: Georgie, Geena, Gigi, Gina, Ina.

**Geraldine**: From the Old German meaning 'spear-ruler' or the Irish Gaelic meaning 'one of the Fitzgeralds'. Short form: Geri, Gerry, Jerry.

**Germaine**: From the French meaning 'German'; see also Gemma. Alternative spelling: Jermaine.

**Gertrude**: From the German *gar* or *ger* meaning spear and *ßruß* meaning 'strength'. Alternative spellings: Geerta, Geertuida, Gertraud, Gertrudis. Short forms: Gerta, Gertha, Gertie, Gerty, Trudi, Trudie, Trudy.

**Getha**: See Gertrude.

**Ghislaine**: From the French meaning 'pledge' or 'hostage'. Alternative spelling: Ghislane.

**Gigi**: From Gilberte.

**Gilberte**: The feminine form of Gilbert (see Boys' Names).

**Gilda**: From the English meaning 'to gild'.

**Gillian:** Feminie form of Julian (see Boys' Names). Alternative spellings: Jillian, Juliana. Short forms: Gill, Gilly, Jill, Jilly.

**Gina:** See Georgina and Regina. Alternative spelling: Geena.

**Ginger:** See Virginia.

**Ginny:** See Virginia.

**Giselle:** From the Old German word gisil meaning 'pledge' or the Anglo-Saxon meaning 'sword'. Alternative spellings: Gisela, Gisèle, Gisell.

**Gita:** From the Sanskrit meaning 'song'. Alternative spelling: Geeta.

**Giulia:** See Julia.

**Gladys:** From the Welsh meaning 'ruler' or possibly from the Latin meaning 'a small sword'. Alternative spelling: Gwladys. Short forms: Gladdie, Glads.

**Glenda:** From the Welsh meaning 'holy' or 'good'.

**Glenis:** See Glenys.

**Glenys:** From the Welsh meaning 'holy'. Alternative spellings: Glenis, Glennis, Glennys.

**Gloria:** From the Latin meaning 'glory'. Alternative spellings: Glorianna, Glorianne, Glory.

**Glynis:** From the Welsh meaning 'little valley'.

**Grace:** From the Latin meaning 'thanks', 'graceful' or 'lovely'. Alternative spelling: Gracie.

**Gráinne:** From the Irish Gaelic meaning 'love'.

**Greta:** See Margaret.

**Gretchen**: See Margaret.

**Guenevere**: See Genevieve. Alternative spelling: Guinevere.

**Gwen**: From the Welsh meaning 'white'.

**Gwenda**: From the Welsh meaning 'good' or 'fair'.

**Gwendalen**: From the Welsh meaning 'white circle'.

**Gwendolyn**: See Genvieve. Alternative spelling: Gwendolen. Short forms: Gwen, Gwena, Gwenda, Gwendi, Gwinn, Gwynn, Wenda, Wendie, Wendoline, Wendy.

**Gwyneth**: From the Welsh meaning 'blessed'. Alternative spelling: Gwynedd. Short forms: Gwen, Gwyn.

## H

**Hadassah**: From the Hebrew meaning 'myrtle tree'. Alternative spellings: Esther, Laurel.

**Hadria**: A feminine form of Hardian (see Boys' Names).

**Haf**: From the Welsh meaning 'summer'.

**Haley**: Old English *heg* meaning 'hay' and *leah* meaning 'clearing' or the Norse *haela* meaning 'hero'. Alternative spellings: Haile, Hailey, Hallie, Hayley.

**Hannah**: From the Hebrew meaning 'God has favoured me'. Alternative spelling: Hana, Hanna, Nancy.

**Harmony**: From the Greek meaning 'concord' or 'in agreement'. Alternative spellings: Harmonia, Harmonie.

**Harriet**: See Henrietta. Alternative spellings: Harriette.

**Hayley:** See Haley.

**Hazel:** From the Old English *haesel* meaning 'hazelnut'.

**Heather:** From the plant of the same name.

**Heaven-lee:** Origins for the use of this as a name are uncertain but it has suddenly begun to appear as a name. Alternative spelling: Heavenly.

**Heidi:** From the Old German meaning 'proud' or 'noble'.

**Helen:** From the Greek *helios* meaning 'sun' or *elene* meaning 'bright one' or 'light'. Alternative spellings: Aileen, Ailie, Eileen, Eileigh, Elaine, Elana, Elane, Elanor, Elanora, Eleanor, Eleanore, Elen, Elena, Elenora, Elin, Elinor, Elle, Ellen, Elli, Ellie, Elly, Ellyn, Ellynn, Hela, Helaine, Heleen, Helen, Helena, Helene, Helina, Ilana, Ileanna, Ilena, Iliana, Ilona, Ilonka, Illuska, Lana, Leen, Leentje, Lena, Leni, Lenka, Lenore, Leona, Leonora, Leonore, Leora, Liana, Lina, Nell, Nelli, Nellie, Nelly, Nora, Olena, Olenka, Yelena.

**Helena:** See Helen.

**Helga:** From the Norse meaning 'holy'. Alternative spelling: Elga, Olga, Olenka.

**Heloise:** See Louise. Alternative spelling: Eloise.

**Henrietta:** The female form of Henry (See Boys' Names). Short forms: Harriet, Harry, Hattie, Hettie, Hetty.

**Hera:** From the Greek meaning 'queen' or 'jealous'.

**Hermia:** From the Greek meaning 'messenger'.

**Hermina:** From the Latin meaning 'noble'.

**Hermione:** From the Greek meaning 'earthly' or 'messenger'. Alternative spellings: Hermine, Herminia.

**Hero:** From the Greek meaning 'hero'.

**Hesper:** From the Greek *hesperos* meaning 'evening' or 'evening star'. Alternative spelling: Hespera.

**Hester:** See Esther.

**Heulwen:** From the Welsh meaning 'sunshine'.

**Hilda:** From the Old English meaning 'battle'. Alternative spellings: Hildemar. Short forms: Hilde, Hildi, Hidie, Hildy, Hylda.

**Hillary:** From the Latin *hilarius* meaning 'cheerful'. Alternative spellings: Hilaire, Hilarie, Hilary.

**Hollie:** From the plant of the same name. Alternative spelling: Holly.

**Honey:** From the Old English meaning 'honey' or 'nectar'; see also Honor.

**Honor:** From the Latin meaning 'acknowledgement', 'recognition', .Alternative spellings: Honey, Honora, Honoria, Horeen, Nora, Norah, Onora.

**Hope:** From the Old English meaning 'optimism'.

**Hyacinth:** From the Greek meaning 'precious blue stone' or the flower. Alternative spellings: Cynthia, Hyacinthe, Jacenta, Jacinda, Jacinta, Jacinthe, Jackie, Jackey, Jacky.

## I

**Ianthe**: From the Greek meaning 'violet flower'. Alternative spelling: Iolanthe.

**Ida:** From the Old German *id* meaning 'work' or the Old English meaning 'protection' or 'possession'. Alternative spellings: Aida, Ide, Ita.

**Idris**: From the Welsh meaning 'impulsive Lord'.

**Igrayne**: According to the legend, Igrayne was the mother of King Arthur, the meaning is unknown. Alternative spellings: Igraine, Ygraine, Ygrayne.

**Ilana**: From the Hebrew meaning 'tree'. Alternative spelling: Ilona.

**Ilona**: Possibly from the Hungarian meaning 'beauty'; see also Helen or Ilana. Alternative spellings: Ilana, Ilonka. Short form: Ili.

**Ilse**: See Elizabeth.

**Iman**: From the Arabic *iman* meaning 'faith' or 'belief' or *amana* meaning 'to believe'. Alternative spelling: Imani.

**Imelda**: From the Latin meaning 'wishful'.

**Imogen**: Possibly from the Gaelic *inghean* meaning 'girl' or 'maiden' or the Latin meaning 'blameless', 'innocent', 'likeness' or 'image'. Alternative spellings: Immogen, Imogene. Short forms: Imo, Genie.

**Ina**: See Georgina or Christina.

**India**: After the sub-continent. Short form: Indy.

**Indiana**: After the American state. Short form: Indy.

**Indira:** From the Sanskrit meaning 'splendid'. Short form: Indy.

**Inez:** From the Spanish meaning 'chaste'. Alternative spelling: Ines.

**Inga:** See Ingrid. Alternative spelling: Inge.

**Inge:** Possibly from the Norse meaning 'meadow'; see also Inga.

**Ingrid:** From the Norwegian meaning 'Ing's ride', Ing being the Norse god of fertility and crops who rode on a boar. Alternative spellings: Inga.

**Innes:** From the Gaelic meaning 'island'.

**Iolanthe:** See Ianthe.

**Iona:** From the Scottish island in the Hebrides of the same name, possibly from the Old Norse meaning 'island'.

**Ione:** Possibly from the Greek meaning 'violet'.

**Irene:** From the Greek *eirene* meaning 'peace'. Alternative spellings: Irina, Eireen.

**Iris:** From the Greek meaning 'rainbow' or from the flower.

**Irma:** From the German meaning 'whole'.

**Isabelle:** See Elizabeth. Alternative spellings: Isabel, Isabella, Isobel, Iseabail, Isbel, Ysabel. Short form: Bella, Isa, Issi, Issie, Issy, Sabelle.

**Isadora:** From the Greek meaning 'gift of Iris'. Alternative spelling: Isidora.

**Iseult:** See Isolde.

**Isla:** From the Scottish island Islay. Alternative spelling: Ila.

**Isola:** From the Latin meaning 'isolated' or 'alone'.

**Isolde:** Possibly from the Welsh *esyllt* meaning 'fair one' or the Old High German meaning 'to rule'. Alternative spellings: Iseult, Isolda, Yseult.

**Ita:** From the Old Irish meaning 'thirst' or 'desire for truth'.

**Ivana:** A feminine form of John (see Boys' Names).

**Ivette:** See Yvette.

**Ivy:** From the plant of the same name.

## J

**Jacaline:** See Jacqueline.

**Jacinda:** See Hyacinth. Alternative spellings: Jacinta, Jacinthe.

**Jacqueline:** A feminine form of James (see Boys' Names). Alternative spellings: Jacaline, Jackalyn, Jacquelyn, Jacquetta. Jaqueline. Short forms: Jackey, Jacki, Jackie, Jacksie, Jacksey, Jacky, Jacqui.

**Jade:** From the Latin meaning 'fierce' or from the precious stone. Alternative spellings: Jayde.

**Jael:** From the Hebrew meaning 'antelope' or 'mountain goat'.

**Jaime:** A feminine form of James (see Boys' Names) or from the French meaning 'I love'.

**Jalila:** From the Arabic meaning 'great' or 'illustrious'.

**Jamie:** A feminine form of James (See Boys' Names).

**Jamilah:** From the Arabic meaning 'beautiful' or 'elegant'. Alternative spelling: Jamila.

**Jan**: See Janet.

**Jana**: See Janet.

**Jane**: Feminine form of John (see Boys' Names). Alternative spellings: Ivana, Jan, Jana, Janae, Janean, Janeen, Janel, Janela, Janella, Janelle, Janessa, Janet, Janeta, Janetta, Janette, Janey, Janka, Jani, Janica, Janice, Janie, Janina, Janine, Janis, Janita, Janith, Janna, Jannelle, Jany, Jayne, Jaynie, Jean, Jeanne, Jeanette, Jeani, Jeanie, Jeanine, Jehane, Jene, Jenni, Jennie, Jenny, Jess, Jessi, Jessie, Jessy, Jinni, Jinnie, Jinny, Joan, Joana, Joanne, Joeann, Johanna, Joni, Jonie, Jony, Jovanna, Seonaid, Sheena, Sian, Sinéad, Siobhán.

**Janeil**: Possibly a variation on the name Janelle which is a combination of Jane and Danielle.

**Janet**: A Scottish form of Jane derived from the French form Jeannette. Alternative spellings: Jan, Janella, Janelle, Janete, Janetta, Janette, Janot, Nettie, Netta, Seonaid.

**Janelle**: See Jane.

**Janice**: See Janet.

**Janis**: See Jane.

**Jasmine**: From the Persian or Arabic *yasmin* meaning 'an olive flower'. Alternative spellings: Jasmin, Jasmina, Jesmond, Jessamine, Jessamy, Jessie, Yasmin, Yasmina, Yasmine.

**Jean**: See Jane. Short forms: Jeni, Jenny, Gene, Genie, Jeane, Jeanette, Jeanie, Jeanne, Jeannette, Jeannine.

**Jeanette**: French derivative of Jean.

**Jeanine**: From the Old French name Jehanne, a form of Jane.

**Jemima**: From the Hebrew meaning 'dove'. Alternative spellings: Jemimah. Short forms: Jem, Jemma, Mima.

**Jemma**: See Gemma or Jemima.

**Jenna**: Possibly from Jennifer.

**Jennifer**: From the Celtic meaning 'fair' and 'yielding'. Possibly also from the names Guenivere, Genevieve or Gwendolyn. Alternative spellings: Jenfer, Jenifer. Short forms: Jen, Jeni, Jennie, Jenny, Jinny.

**Jermaine**: See Germaine.

**Jessica**: From the Hebrew meaning 'he beholds' or 'the rich one'. Alternative spellings: Jesika, Jessika. Short forms: Jess, Jessie, Jessy, Jessye.

**Jessie**: From the Hebrew *yishai* meaning 'riches' or 'a gift', see also Jessica. Alternative spellings: Jessi, Jessey.

**Jet**: From the French *jaiet* meaning 'black gem stone'. Alternative spelling: Jetta.

**Jewel**: From the French meaning 'gemstone'. Alternative spelling: Jewell.

**Jezebel**: From the Hebrew meaning 'impure'.

**Jill**: The short form of Jillian.

**Jillian**: See Gillian. Short form: Jilly, Jill.

**Jinny**: See Virginia.

**Jo**: Short form of Joanna or Josephine.

**Joan**: See Jane. Alternative spellings: Henise, Janis, Janna, Jean, Joana, Joann, Joanne, Joeann, Johan, Johna, Jonet, Joni, Jonie, Jovana, Juana, Juanita. Short form: Joanie.

**Joann**: See Joan. Alternative spellings: Joane, Joanna, Jo-Anne, Joanne. Short forms Jo, Joey.

**Jobina**: From the Hebrew meaning 'persecuted'.

**Jocasta**: From the Italian meaning 'light-hearted'.

**Jocelyn**: From the Latin meaning 'cheerful' or 'sportive'; the Celtic name Josse meaning 'champion' or the Old German meaning 'descendant of the Goths'. Alternative spellings: Jocelin, Joceline, Jocelyn, Jocelyne, Joscelin, Joscelind, Josceline, Joscelyn, Josette, Josie, Joslyn. Short forms: Jo, Joey, Josie, Josey.

**Jocosa**: From the Old English meaning 'merry'.

**Jodie**: See Judith. Alternative spelling: Jodi, Jody.

**Joella**: From the French name Joëlle, which is the feminine form of Joel (see Boys' Names). Alternative spelling: Joelle.

**Johanna**: See Jane or Joan.

**Jolie**: From the French meaning 'pretty one'.

**Joline**: From the Hebrew meaning 'she will increase'. Alternative spelling: Jolene.

**Joni**: See Joan. Alternative spelling: Joani.

**Jordan**: From the Hebrew meaning 'flowing down'. Alternative spellings: Jordain, Jordaine, Jordann, Jorden, Jordin, Jordyn.

**Jordana**: From the Hebrew meaning 'the descending'. Alternative spelling: Jordanna.

**Jorie**: A feminine form of George (see Boys' Names).

**Jorita**: From the Latin *jovalis* meaning 'joyful'.

**Joscelyn**: See Jocelyn.

**Josephine**: A feminine form of Joseph (see Boys' Names). Alternative spellings: Josephina. Short forms: Fifi, Jo, Joey, Josette, Josie, Posey.

**Josette**: See Josephine.

**Josipa**: Possibly a feminine form of Joseph (see Boys' Names). Alternative spelling: Josepha.

**Joy**: From the Latin jocosa meaning 'merry'.

**Joyce**: From the Latin meaning 'joyous' or the English meaning 'cheerful' or 'merry'. Alternative spellings: Joice, Joisse, Joice. Short forms: Joy, Josie, Jo.

**Juanita**: See Joan. Short form: Nita.

**Judith**: From the Hebrew meaning 'praised'. Alternative spelling: Judit. Short forms: Jodie, Judi, Judie, Judy.

**Julia**: A feminine form of Julius (see Boys' Names). Alternative spellings: Gillian, Gillie, Giulia, Juillia, Julca, Julcia, Juli, Juliana, Juliane, Julianna, Julie, Juliet, Julieta, Julietta, Julina, Juline, Julinka, Juliska, Julissa, Julita, Julka. Short form: Jul, Jula, Julie.

**Juliana**: See Julia.

**Julie**: A French form of Julia.

**Juliet**: See Julia. Alternative spellings: Julliette, Juliette, Jullietta, Julietta.

**June**: From the the month or from the Latin *juvenior* meaning 'young'.

**Juniper**: From the plant.

**Juno**: From the Latin meaning 'queen'.

**Justina**: From the Latin Justus meaning 'justice'.

**Justine**: From the Latin meaning 'just'.

## K

**Kaci**: From the Irish meaning 'vigilant'. Alternative spellings: Kacie, Casey, Cayce.

**Kaela:** From the Hebrew or Arabic meaning 'beloved sweetheart'.

**Kai**: From the Hawaiian meaning 'sea'.

**Kaila**: From the Hebrew meaning 'laurel crown'. Alternative spelling: Kayla, Kallie.

**Kaitlin**: See Catherine. Alternative spellings: Kaitlyn, Caitlin.

**Kaley**: See Kay. Alternative spellings: Kayleigh, Kailey.

**Kallie**: See Kaila.

**Kallista**: From the Greek meaning 'beautiful'. Alternative spelling: Callista.

**Kameron**: See Cameron.

**Kara**: See Catherine.

**Karen**: See Catherine. Alternative spellings: Caryn, Karan, Karin, Karina, Karon, Karren, Karrin, Karyn, Keren, Koren.

**Karesa**: See Catherine.

**Karina**: See Catherine.

**Karis**: From the Greek meaning 'grace'.

**Karisma**: From the Greek meaning 'favour' or 'grace'.

**Karly**: See Carly.

**Karrie**: See Carrie. Alternative spellings: Kari.

**Kasey**: A feminine form of Casey (see Boys' Names).

**Kassady**: See Cassidy. Alternative spellings: Cassidy, Kassidy.

**Kassandra**: See Cassandra.

**Kassidy**: See Cassidy.

**Kassie**: See Cassie.

**Katarina**: See Catherine.

**Katelyn**: See Caitlin.

**Katherine**: See Catherine.

**Kathleen**: See Caitlin or Catherine. Alternative spelling: Kathleena, Kathlena, Kathlene, Kathlyn, Kathlynn.

**Kathy**: See Catherine.

**Katie**: See Catherine. Alternative spelling: Kat, Kata, Kate, Katee, Katey, Kati, Katia, Katianne, Katinka, Katt, Katy, Katya.

**Katrina**: See Catherine. Alternative spelling: Katrin, Katrine. Short form: Trina.

**Kay**: From the English or Scandinavian meaning 'keeper of the keys'. Alternative spellings: Cayla, Kayla, Kaylee.

**Keegan**: From the Irish-Gaelic meaning 'little fierce one'.

**Keeley**: From the Irish-Gaelic meaning 'good-looking', 'lively' or 'aggressive'.

**Keira**: A feminine form of Kier (see Boys' Names).

**Kelan**: From the Irish name Caolán meaning 'slender'.

**Kelly**: From the Irish meaning 'lively' or 'aggressive'. Alternative spellings: Kelley, Kelleigh, Kelli.

**Kelsie**: From the English meaning 'brave'. Alternative spelling: Kelsey.

**Kendra**: From the Old English meaning 'wise' or 'all-knowing'. Alternative spelling: Kindra.

**Kerby**: See Kirby.

**Keren**: From the Hebrew meaning 'beauty'; see also Karen. Alternative spellings: Kerrin, Keryn.

**Kerensa**: From the Cornish *cres* meaning 'peace' and *ha* meaning 'love'.

**Kerry**: From the Irish Gaelic meaning 'dusky' or 'dark'. Alternative spellings: Kerri, Kerrie.

**Kezia**: From the Hebrew meaning 'sweet smelling spice'. Alternative spelling: Keziah. Short form: Kezzie.

**Khayla**: See Michaela.

**Khristina**: See Christina.

**Kiara**: See Ciara. Alternative spellings: Kiera, Kira.

**Kiera**: The feminine form of Kieran (see Boys' Names). Alternative spellings: Ciara, Ciera, Keara, Keira, Kieran, Kierran.

**Kim**: From the Old English meaning 'royally born'. Alternative spelling: Kym.

**Kimberley**: From the Old English meaning 'king's wood'. Alternative spellings: Kimberlee, Kimberleigh, Kimberli, Kymberlie, Kimberlin, Kimberlyn, Kymberley.

**Kindra**: See Kendra.

**Kinsey**: From the Old Norse *kyn* meaning 'family'.

**Kira**: From Greek *cyrus* meaning 'sun' or the Russian meaning 'lady'; see also Ciara.

**Kirby**: From the English meaning 'church farm'. Alternative spelling: Kerby.

**Kirstin**: See Christina. Alternative spellings: Kerstin, Kiersten, Kierstin, Kierston, Kirsten, Kirstine, Kirstyn, Kyrstin.

**Kirsty**: See Christina.

**Kitty**: See Katherine.

**Klarissa**: See Clarissa.

**Konstance**: See Constance.

**Kora**: See Cora.

**Korina**: See Corinna.

**Krista**: See Christine.

**Kristen**: See Christine.

**Kristi:** See Christine.

**Kristin:** See Christine.

**Kristina:** See Christine.

**Krystal:** From the Greek *krystallos* meaning 'ice'; see also Crystal. Alternative spelling: Krystle.

**Kyla:** From the Gaelic *caol* meaning 'narrow'.

**Kyle:** From the Gaelic Irish meaning 'narrow strip of land' or the Yiddish meaning 'crowned with laurel'.

**Kylie:** From the Aboriginal meaning 'curved stick' (boomerang).

**Kyra:** From the Greek meaning 'lady'.

**Kyria:** From the Greek meaning 'lord' or 'god'.

## L

**Lacey:** From the English meaning 'lace'. Alternative spelling: Lacy.

**Laetita:** See Letitia.

**Laila:** From the Persian meaning 'night' or 'dark-haired'. Alternative spellings: Laili, Laleh, Layla.

**Lalita:** From the Sanskrit meaning 'charming' or possibly from the Arabic meaning 'she who plays'.

**Lana:** See Alana.

**Lani:** From the Hawaiian meaning 'sky'.

**Lara:** From the Latin meaning 'famous' or 'protection'; see also Larissa.

**Larissa:** Possibly from the Latin *lascivia* meaning 'playfulness' or 'jollity' or the Greek meaning 'cheerful'. Alternative spellings: Larisa, Laris, Lissa. Short form: Lara.

**Laura**: From the Latin meaning 'laurel'. Alternative spellings: Laurie, Loretta.

**Laurel**: From the Greek meaning 'strength' or 'courage' or the English meaning 'laurel tree'. Alternative spelling: Lorel.

**Lauren**: From the Latin *lawrentium* meaning 'the place of the laurel trees' or 'laurel crowned'. Alternative spellings: Lauryn, Loren, Lorena.

**Laurie**: See Laura.

**Lavender**: From the plant.

**Laverne**: From the French meaning 'woodland'.

**Lavinia**: From the Latin meaning 'woman of Rome'. Alternative spelling: Lavina. Short forms: Vin, Vinia, Vinnie, Vinny.

**Layla**: See Laila or Lila.

**Lea**: From the Old English meaning 'field' or 'meadow'. Alternative spelling: Lee, Leigh.

**Leah**: From the Hebrew meaning 'weak eyes' or 'languid'. Alternative spellings: Lea, Leia, Leigh, Lia.

**Leandra**: From the Greek meaning 'lionness'.

**Leanne**: See Lianne.

**Leanora**: See Eleanor.

**Lee**: From the Irish meaning 'poetic' or the Chinese meaning 'plum'; see also Lea, Leah. Alternative spelling: Leigh.

**Leena:** From the Sanskrit meaning 'devoted; see also Helen. Alternative spelling: Lena.

**Leia:** See Leah.

**Leila:** From the Persian meaning 'night'. Alternative spellings: Leilah, Lila.

**Leilani:** From the Hawaiian *lani* meaning 'heavenly' or 'of the sky' and *lei* meaning flower' thus 'heavenly flower'.

**Lenere:** From the Latin meaning 'peacemaker'.

**Lenore:** See Eleanor. Short form: Nora.

**Leona:** See Leonie.

**Leonie:** From the Greek *leon* or the Latin *leo* meaning 'lion'. Alternative spellings: Leona, Leontine, Leontina. Short forms: Leo.

**Leonore:** See Eleanor.

**Leontine:** See Leonie. Alternative spelling: Leontina. Short forms: Leo.

**Lesley:** Female version of Leslie (see Boys' Names). Alternative spelling: Leslee. Short form: Lee.

**Letitia:** From the Latin meaning 'gladness' or 'joyfulness'. Alternative spellings: Laeticia, Laetitia, Lettice. Short forms: Laeta, Letty, Tia,Tisha.

**Lia:** From the Greek meaning 'bringer of good news' see also Leah.

**Lianne:** From the Greek *helios* meaning 'sun'; the Latin meaning 'youth' or the English meaning 'meadow'. Alternative spellings:

Leanne, Lian, Liana, Liane, Lianna.

**Libby**: See Elizabeth.

**Liberty**: From the Latin meaning 'free'.

**Liese**: See Elizabeth.

**Liesel**: See Elizabeth. Alternative spelling: Liesl.

**Lila**: From the Hebrew meaning 'night'. Alternative spellings: Lilah, Liliah, Layla, Laylah.

**Lilian**: From the Latin meaning 'lily'. Alternative spelling: Lillian.

**Lilith**: From the Arabic meaning 'of the night'.

**Linda**: Possibly from the German meaning 'linden tree'; possibly the Spanish *linda* meaning 'pretty' or possibly a short form of names ending in -lind , meaning 'weak', 'tender' or 'soft'. Short forms: Lin, Lyn.

**Lindsay**: See Boys' Names. Alternative spellings: Lindsey, Linsey.

**Linnet**: From the Welsh meaning 'bird'. Alternative spellings: Llinos, Lynette.

**Lisa**: From the French meaning 'blessed' or 'gifted'; see also Elizabeth.

**Lisanne**: Combination of Lisa and Anne.

**Lisette**: See Elizabeth.

**Liv**: See Olivia.

**Livia**: See Olivia.

**Liz**: See Elizabeth.

**Liza**: See Elizabeth.

**Llinos**: See Linnet.

**Logan**: From the Scottish meaning 'low meadow' or possibly after the Scottish place of the same name in Ayrshire.

**Lois**: From the Greek meaning 'good' or 'desirable'.

**Lola**: See Carlotta, Dolores or Louise.

**Lolita**: See Dolores.

**Loni**: See Alona.

**Lonita**: From the Spanish meaning 'little one'.

**Lorelei**: From the German meaning 'song' or 'alluring'.

**Lorena**: See Lauren.

**Loretta**: See Laura. Alternative spelling: Lauretta.

**Lorna**: From the Scottish place name. Alternative spellings: Lorne, Lorn.

**Lorraine**: From the Latin meaning 'full of sorrow' or from the French region. Alternative spellings: Laraine, Loraine. Short form: Lori.

**Lottie**: See Charlotte.

**Lotty**: See Charlotte.

**Louisa**: From the French meaning 'famous'. Short form: Lulu.

**Louise**: From the French meaning 'famous'. Short forms: Lola, Lou, Louie, Louella, Luella.

**Lourdes**: From the French town.

**Lucia**: From the Italian meaning 'light'. Alternative spellings: Lucilla, Lucille, Lucina.

**Lucinda**: From the Latin meaning 'light'. Short form: Cindy.

**Lucretia**: Female version of the Roman family name Lucretius, possibly from the Latin meaning 'rich' or 'rewarded'. Alternative spelling: Lucrezia.

**Lucy**: From the Latin meaning 'light'.

**Ludmilla**: From the Slav meaning 'people' and 'grace'.

**Luella**: See Louise.

**Lydia**: From the Greek meaning 'a native of Lydia', an ancient city in Aisa Minor.

**Lyn**: Possibly from the Old English meaning 'dweller by the waterfall'; see also Linda. Alternative spellings: Lin, Lina, Linn, Linne, Lynette, Lynn.

**Lynette**: Possibly from the Welsh name Eluned from *elynid* meaning 'idol'; see also Linnet.

**Lynsey**: See Lindsay.

**Lyric**: From the Greek *lurikos* meaning 'to express thoughts or feelings'.

**Lysandra**: The feminine form of Lysander (see Boys' Names).

## M

**Mab**: See Mabel.

**Mabel**: From the French *ma belle* meaning 'my beautiful one' or the Latin meaning 'worthy of love'. Alternative spellings: Amabel, Mabell, Mabelle. Short forms: Mab, Mabb.

**Mackenzie**: See Boys' Names.

**Maddy**: See Madeleine.

**Madeleine**: The French form of Magdalene. Alternative spellings: Madaleine, Madaline, Madalyn, Madelaine, Madelin, Madelina, Madeline, Madella. Short forms: Maddy, Madge, Mads, Laine.

**Madigan**: See Magdalena.

**Madison**: Possibly from Magdalen; from the American surname or the Old English meaning 'son of Maud'. Short forms: Maddy, Maddie.

**Madonna**: From the Italian name for the Virgin Mary or the Italian meaning 'my Lady'. Short form: Maddy, Madge, Maddie, Mads.

**Mae**: See May.

**Maegan**: See Megan.

**Maelona**: From the Welsh meaning 'princess'.

**Maeve**: From the Irish Gaelic *meadhbh* meaning 'intoxicating' or 'joyous'; see also Mavis. Alternative spellings: Maive, Mave, Meave, Meaveen.

**Magda**: See Magdalena.

**Magdalen**: See Magdalena.

**Magdalena**: From the Greek meaning 'high tower'. Alternative spellings: Madigan, Magdalina, Magdelana, Magdalen. Short form: Magda, Malena.

**Magdalene**: From the Hebrew meaning 'high tower' or possibly 'woman of Magdala' – Magdala being a town on the Sea of Galilee; Alternative spellings: Magdalen, Madalena, Madeleine, Madeline, Madella, Madelon, Magdalen, Magdalena, Magdaline, Marlena, Marlene, Maudlin, Migdana. Short forms: Leli, Lena, Lenna, Lina, Mada, Madge, Magda, Maggie.

**Maggie**: From the Hebrew meaning 'pearl'; see Magdalene, Margaret.

**Magnolia**: Possibly from the Latin meaning 'flowering tree' or from the flower of the same name.

**Mahalia**: From the Hebrew meaning 'tenderness'.

**Maliha**: From the Arabic meaning 'nice' or 'good'.

**Mai**: From the Welsh meaning 'May'.

**Maia**: See Maya.

**Mair**: A Welsh form of Mary.

**Maire**: See Mary.

**Mairead**: From the Gaelic Irish meaning 'magistrate' or 'judge'.

**Mairi**: A Gaelic version of Mary.

**Mairin**: A Gaelic version of Mary.

**Maisie**: See Margaret. Alternative spellings: Maisey, Maisy, Maysie, Mazie.

**Mala**: From the French meaning 'ill' or 'bad'.

**Malea**: From the Hawaiian meaning 'flower'; Alternative spelling: Melia.

**Malena**: See Magdalen. Alternative spelling: Malina.

**Malka**: From the Hebrew meaning 'queen'. Alternative spelling: Malkah.

**Mallory**: From the French meaning 'unfortunate' or possibly from the Old German meaning 'an army counsellor'. Alternative spellings: Mallary, Malerie, Mallery, Malloree, Mallorey, Mellory. Short forms: Mallie, Mally.

**Malvina**: From the Gaelic meaning 'smooth brow'. Alternative spelling: Melvina.

**Maime**: From the French meaning 'my sweetheart'.

**Manda**: See Amanda.

**Mandara**: From the Hindi meaning 'calm'.

**Mandy**: From the Latin meaning 'loved'; see also Amanda. Alternative spellings: Mandi, Mandee, Mandie.

**Manon**: See Mary.

**Mara**: From the Hebrew meaning 'bitter'; see Mary.

**Marcella**: A feminine form of Marcel (see Boys' Names). Alternative spellings: Marcela, Marcell, Marcelle, Marcelline, Marcello, Marcena, Marsella. Short forms: Cellie, Celly, Marcie, Marcy, Marsha.

**Marcia**: A feminine form of Marcus (see Boys' Names) Short forms: Marci, Marcie, Marcy, Marsha, Mercia.

**Mare**: From the Latin meaning 'the sea'. Alternative spelling: Maire.

**Margaret**: From the Hebrew *margaron* meaning 'pearl'. Alternative spellings: Margarita, Margery, Margot, Marguerite, Marquette. Mereid. Short forms: Daisy, Greta, Gretchen, Madge, Maggie, Mags, Maisie, Mamie, Margo, Margot, Meg, Megan, Meggie, Mog, Peg, Pegeen, Peggy, Polly, Rita.

**Margarita**: From the Spanish meaning 'daisy'. Alternative spellings: Margaux, Margo, Margot, Marguerita.

**Margaux**: See Margarita. Alternative spellings: Margot, Margo.

**Margery**: See Margaret. Short forms: Marg, Margie, Marj, Marjie.

**Margo**: See Margaret or Margaux.

**Mari**: See Mary.

**Maria**: See Mary. Short forms: Mimi, Ria.

**Mariah**: See Mary.

**Mariam**: From the Hebrew meaning either 'sea of bitterness' or 'child of our wishes'; See also Mary.

**Marian**: See Mary. Alternative spelling: Marianna, Marianne, Maryanne.

**Maribel**: From the French meaning 'beautiful Mary'. Alternative spellings: Marabel, Marbelle, Maribell, Maribella, Maribelle.

**Marie**: See Mary.

**Mariel**: See Mary. Alternative spelling: Mariella.

**Marieta**: From the Italian meaning 'grace and beauty'. Alternative spellings: Marietta, Maretta, Marrietta.

**Marigold**: From the Old English meaning 'Mary's gold' or from the flower. Alternative spelling: Marygold.

**Marilla**: See Mary.

**Marilyn**: Possibly from Mary meaning 'Mary's line' or possibly a blend of Mary and Ellen or Lynn. Alternative spellings: Maralyn, Marlyn, Marilee, Marilynn, Marylyn, Merill.

**Marina**: From the Latin meaning 'of the sea'. Alternative spelling: Mare, Maris, Marisa, Marissa, Marne, Marni, Marnie, Marnina, Marys, Rina.

**Marion**: See Mary.

**Marisa**: From the Latin meaning 'a gem', 'a special one' or 'of the sea' or the Hebrew meaning 'summit'. Alternative spellings: Marijse, Marissa. Short form: Marie.

**Marjorie**: See Margery.

**Marla**: See Marlene.

**Marlene**: See Magdalene.

**Marlo**: See Mary. Alternative spellings: Marlow, Marlowe .

**Marlyse**: See Mary.

**Marnie**: See Marina. Alternative spellings: Marni, Marnia.

**Marquette**: See Margaret. Alternative spellings: Markette, Marquita.

**Marsha**: See Marcia or Marcella.

**Martha**: From the Aramaic meaning 'lady'. Alternative spellings: Marta, Martelle, Marthe, Mattie, Matty.

**Martina**: From the Latin meaning 'martial' or 'warlike'.

Alternative spellings: Martine, Martelle, Martino. Short forms: Marti, Marty, Marta.

**Martine**: See Martina. Short form: Marti, Marty.

**Marvel**: From the Latin meaning 'full of wonder'. Alternative spellings: Marvella, Marvelle, Marvell.

**Mary**: From the Hebrew name Miriam meaning 'sea of bitterness' or 'O child of our wishes' or the Latin *stella maris* meaning 'star of the sea'. Alternative spellings: Mair, Maire, Mairi, Mairin, Mame, Mamie, Manon, Mara, Marabel, Marella, Mari, Maria, Mariah, Mariam, Marian, Mariana, Marianna, Marice, Maridel, Marie, Mariel, Marietta, Mariette, Marilee, Marilin, Marilla, Marilyn, Marion, Marita, Marlo, Marlyse, Marren, Marya, Maryam, Maryann, Maryanna, Maryanne, Marylin, Marylinn, Marylyn, Maura, Maureen, Maurene, Maurie, May, Meirion, Meri, Meriel, Merrill, Meryl, Mia, Millie, Mimi, Minette, Minni, Minnie, Minny, Miriam, Moira, Molly, Muriel, Muriell, Polli, Pollie, Polly.

**Marysol**: From the Spanish meaning 'ocean' and 'sun'. Alternative spelling: Marisol.

**Masey**: A feminine form of Macey (see Boys' Names).

**Matilda**: From the Old German meaning 'mighty in battle'. Alternative spellings: Mathilda, Maud. Short forms: Matti, Mattie, Matty, Tilda, Tilly.

**Maud**: Variant of Matilda. Alternative spellings: Maude, Maudie.

**Maura**: From the Celtic meaning 'dark'.

**Maureen**: A Gaelic version of Mairin derived from Mary, possibly meaning 'little Mary' or 'little bitter one' or the French meaning 'dark-skinned. Alternative form: Moreen. Short form: Mo.

**Mauve**: From the French meaning 'lilac-coloured'.

**Mave**: See Maeve.

**Mavis**: From the Old English meaning 'song thrush'. Alternative spelling: Maeve.

**Maxime**: From the Latin *maxima* meaning 'greatest'.

**Maxine**: From the Latin meaning 'greatest'. Alternative spellings: Maxeene, Maxene, Maxina. Short forms: Maxie, Maxy.

**May**: From the Latin *Maius* meaning 'the month of May'. Alternative spellings: Mae, Mai.

**Maya**: From the Latin *mai* meaning 'I greet'; after the Roman goddess Maia, the mother of Mercury; the Sanskrit meaning 'illusion' or the Greek meaning 'great'. Alternative spelling: Maia.

**Mechele**: See Michelle.

**Medea**: From the Greek meaning 'ruling' or the Latin meaning 'middle'.

**Medora**: From the Greek meaning 'mother's gift'.

**Meena**: From the Hindi meaning 'bird' or meaning a 'blue precious stone'.

**Meera**: From the Hindi meaning 'saintly woman' or the from the

Hebrew meaning 'light'.

**Meg**: See Margaret.

**Megan**: The Welsh form of Margaret. Alternative spellings: Maegan, Meghan, Meghann, Meighen.

**Meirion**: See Mary.

**Meironwen**: From the Welsh meaning 'white dairymaid'.

**Mel**: See Melanie.

**Melanie**: From the Greek meaning 'black' or 'dark complexion'. Alternative spellings: Melaine, Melana, Melanee, Melonie. Short form: Mel.

**Melantha**: From the Greek meaning 'dark flower'.

**Melia**: See Amelia.

**Melicent**: See Millicent.

**Melinda**: See Melissa. Short form: Mindy.

**Meliora**: From the Latin meaning 'better'.

**Melisande**: See Melissa.

**Melissa**: From the Greek meaning 'honey bee' or the Gaelic name Maoiliosa meaning 'of which is sweet Jesus'. Alternative spellings: Malesa, Melessa, Melinda, Melita, Melitta, Melisande, Missy.

**Melody**: From the Greek meaning 'song' or 'music'. Alternative spellings: Melodi, Melodie.

**Melora**: From the Greek meaning 'golden melon' or 'golden apple'.

**Melvina**: The feminine form of Melvin (see Boys' Names).

**Mena:** From the Dutch or German meaning 'strong'; see also Philomena.

**Mercedes:** From the Spanish name for the Virgin Mary meaning 'Our Lady of Mercies' or the Spanish meaning 'merciful'. Short form: Mercy.

**Mercia:** See Mercy.

**Mercy:** From the Latin *merces* meaning 'reward'; see also Mercedes. Alternative spelling: Mercia, Merilee.

**Mercer:** From the Old English meaning 'merchant'.

**Meredith:** Possibly from the Welsh *Meredudd* meaning 'pretty', 'Lord' or possibly 'from the sea'. Alternative spellings: Meredithe, Meridith. Short form: Merry.

**Mererid:** Welsh version of Margaret.

**Meri:** From the Finnish meaning 'the ocean' or 'the sea' or the Hebrew meaning 'rebellious'.

**Meriel:** From the Gaelic Irish meaning 'shining sea'.

**Merilee:** See Mercy. Alternative spelling: Merrily.

**Merle:** From the French meaning 'blackbird'. Alternative spellings: Meril, Merrill, Merla.

**Merlin:** See Boys' Names.

**Merrill:** See Muriel or Merle.

**Meryl:** See Muriel.

**Mia:** From the Italian meaning 'my'; see also Mary.

**Micah:** A feminine form of Michael (see Boys' Names).

Alternative spellings: Mika, Mycah.

**Michaela**: A feminine form of Michael (see Boys' Names). Alternative spellings: Micaela, Michal, Michala, Michelle, Mikaeli. Short form: Khayla.

**Michal**: See Michaela. Alternative spellings: Michael, Mikal.

**Michelle**: See Michaela. Alternative spellings: Michell, Michella, Mishell, Mishelle. Short forms: Shelly, Shelley.

**Mika**: See Micah.

**Mildred**: From the Old English meaning 'gentle strength'. Short form: Mil, Milda, Millie, Milly, Mindy.

**Milla**: See Camilla.

**Millicent**: From the Old German meaning 'strength' or 'work'. Alternative spelling: Melicent, Melita, Melieta. Short forms: Millie, Milly.

**Millie**: See Millicent.

**Mima**: See Jemima.

**Mimi**: See Maria.

**Mimosa**: From the Latin meaning 'imitative' or the flower.

**Mina**: From the Old German meaning 'love'; the Hindi meaning 'blue sky' or the Arabic meaning 'harbour'. Alternative spellings: Minee, Minna, Minnie, Minny

**Mindy**: See Melinda.

**Minerva**: From the Latin meaning 'wise'. Short form: Minnie, Minnie, Minny.

**Minnie:** See Mina, Minerva or Wilhemina. Alternative spelling: Minny.

**Mira:** From the Spanish meaning 'look'; see also Mirabel.

**Mirabel:** From the Latin meaning 'wonderful'. Alternative spellings: Mirabella, Mirabelle. Short form: Mira.

**Miranda:** Possibly from the Latin *mirari* meaning 'admirable' or 'lovely' or the Latin *mirandus* meaning 'astonished' or 'amazed'.

**Miriam:** From the Hebrew name Maryam, linked to Mary, meaning 'star of the sea'.

**Misty:** From the Old English meaning 'clouded' or 'obscured'.

**Mitra:** From the Persian meaning 'bright', as in bright sun.

**Mo:** See Maureen.

**Moira:** Gaelic Irish meaning 'great'; see also Mary. Alternative spelling: Moyra, Myra.

**Molly:** See Mary.

**Mona:** From the Gaelic Irish meaning 'noble','nun' or 'sweet angel'; possibly the Greek meaning 'single'; the Arabic meaning 'wish' or the Old English meaning 'month'

**Monika:** From the Latin meaning 'advisor'. Alternative spellings: Mona, Monica, Monique.

**Montana:** From the Latin meaning 'mountain' or from the American state.

**Mor:** From the Gaelic meaning 'great' or large'.

**Mora:** From the Gaelic meaning 'the sun'.

**Morag:** From the Gaelic meaning 'great' or possibly 'the sun'.

**Moreen:** See Maureen.

**Morgan:** From the Old Welsh meaning 'sea shore' or 'bright sea'.

**Moriah:** From the Hebrew meaning 'god is my teacher'.

**Morna:** From the Gaelic meaning 'beloved'.

**Morven:** From the Irish Gaelic meaning 'mountain peak'.

**Morwenna:** From the Welsh *morwaneg* meaning 'wave of the sea'.

**Moyra:** See Moira.

**Muirne:** From the Gaelic meaning 'beloved'

**Muriel:** From the Irish meaning 'bright sea'; see also Mary. Alternative spellings: Meriel, Merril, Merrill, Merryl, Meryl, Miriel, Murial.

**Myfanwy:** From the Welsh meaning 'my fine one'.

**Myra:** See Moira. Alternative spelling: Mira.

**Myrtle:** From Greek *myrtos* meaning 'myrtle'. Alternative spelling: Myrta.

## N

**Naamah:** From the Hebrew meaning 'loved', 'beautiful' or 'pleasant'. Alternative spelling: Naama.

**Nabila:** From the Arabic meaning 'noble'.

**Nadean:** From the Russian *Nadezhda* meaning 'hope'. Alternative spelling: Nadine.

**Nadia**: From the Russian meaning 'hope'. Alternative spellings: Nadja, Nadya.

**Nadimah**: From the Arabic meaning 'friend'.

**Naia**: From the Greek *naein* meaning 'to flow'.

**Naima**: From the Arabic meaning 'comfortable' or 'tranquil'. Alternative spelling: Naeema.

**Nairne**: From the Scottish Gaelic meaning 'riverside of lime-trees'.

**Nan**: See Anne, Nanette or Nancy.

**Nana**: See Anne or Nanette.

**Nancy**: See Ann or Hannah. Alternative spellings: Nancey, Nanci, Nancie. Short forms: Nan, Nann.

**Nanette**: From the Hebrew meaning 'grace' or 'God has been gracious'. Short forms: Nan, Nana, Netty.

**Naomi**: From the Hebrew or Arabic meaning 'pleasant' or 'pleasantness'. Alternative spellings: Naima, Neema, Noemi, Noemie.

**Nara**: From the Celtic meaning 'happy' or the Old English meaning 'one who is near or dear'.

**Narcissa**: From the Greek *narke* meaning numbness or possibly meaning daffodil. Alternative spellings: Narcisa, Narcisse.

**Nariko**: From the Japanese meaning 'gentle child'.

**Nastasia**: See Anastasia.

**Natalie**: From the Latin *natalis dies* meaning 'birthday'. Alternative spellings: Natalee, Natalia, Nathalie, Natalya, Natasha,

Nathalee, Nathalia, Nathaly. Short forms: Nat, Talya.

**Natalya**: See Natalie. Short forms: Nat, Talya.

**Natasha**: See Natalie. Alternative spellings: Natacha, Natacia, Natasa, Natashea, Natashia, Natashja, Natashka, Natausha, Natisha. Short forms: Stacey, Tasha.

**Neila**: The feminine form of Neil (see Boys' Names). Alternative spellings: Neala, Neely.

**Nelia**: From the Spanish meaning 'yellow'.

**Nell**: See Eleanor, Ellen, or Helen. Alternative spelling: Nelly.

**Nelle**: Possibly from the Greek meaning 'stone'.

**Nena**: See Nina.

**Nereida**: From the Greek meaning 'sea nymph' or 'daughter of Nereus'. Alternative spellings: Nereyda, Nerida, Nerissa, Neysa.

**Nerissa**: See Nereida. Alternative spelling: Neysa.

**Nerys**: From the Welsh possibly meaning 'lordly'.

**Ness**: See Vanessa.

**Nessa**: From the Old Norse meaning 'headland'; see also Vanessa.

**Nesta**: See Agnes.

**Neta**: Possibly from the Hebrew meaning 'plant' or 'shrub'.

**Netta**: See Annette. Alternative spelling: Nettie.

**Ngaio**: From the Maori meaning 'clever'.

**Nia**: See Niamh.

**Niamh**: From the Irish meaning 'bright'. Short form: Nia.

**Nicole**: The feminine form of Nicholas (see Boys' Names).

Alternative spellings: Niccole, Nichol, Nichola, Nichole, Nicholle, Nicholette, Nickole, Nicola, Nikkole, Nikole, Nycole. Short forms: Nicci, Nickey, Nicki, Nickie, Nicky, Nike, Niki, Nikia, Nikita, Nikkie, Nikki, Niquie.

**Nicolette**: See Nichole. Alternative spelling: Nickolette.

**Nigella**: The feminine form of Nigel (see Boys' Names).

**Nike**: From the Greek meaning 'victorious'.

**Niki**: See Nichole or Nikita.

**Nikita**: From the Greek name Aniketos meaning 'unconquerable'. Short form: Niki, Nikki.

**Nina**: From the Spanish meaning 'little girl'; see also Antonia. Alternative spellings: Neena, Nena.

**Ninon**: See Anne.

**Niquie**: See Nichole.

**Nirvana**: From the Hindi meaning 'heaven' or 'the extinguishing of a fire'.

**Nisha**: From the Hindi meaning 'night'.

**Nissa**: From the Hebrew *nes* meaning 'sign' or 'emblem'.

**Nita**: See Anita and Juanita.

**Nitza**: From the Hebrew meaning 'flower bud'. Alternative spelling: Nitzana.

**Noelle**: The feminine form of Noel (see Boys' Names). Alternative spellings: Noel, Noele, Noella.

**Nola**: See Fenella.

**Nona:** From the Latin meaning 'nine'. Alternative spellings: Noni, Nonie.

**Noor:** From the Arabic meaning 'light'.

**Nora:** See Leonora or Honora. Alternative spelling: Norah.

**Noreen:** See Eleanor.

**Norell:** From the Scandinavian meaning 'from the north'.

**Noriko:** From the Japanese meaning 'law' or 'order'.

**Norma:** From the Latin meaning 'pattern'.

**Nova:** From the Latin meaning 'new'.

**Nuala:** See Fenella.

**Nura:** From the Arabic meaning 'light'.

**Nyela:** From the Arabic name Najla meaning 'beautiful eyes'.

**Nyree:** From the Maori meaning 'sea'.

## O

**Oceana:** From the Greek meaning 'ocean'.

**Octavia:** From the Latin meaning 'eighth'. Alternative spellings: Octaviana, Oktavia. Short forms: Tavi, Tavia, Tavie.

**Odelia:** From the French meaning 'wealthy' or possibly the Hebrew meaning 'I will praise you'. Alternative spellings: Odela, Odella, Odette, Odila, Odile, Ottilie.

**Odessa:** From the Greek meaning 'wandering'.

**Olena:** See Helen.

**Oletha:** See Alethea.

**Olexa**: See Alexandra.

**Olga**: A Russian form of *Helga* meaning 'prosperous' or 'blessed'. Alternative spellings: Elga, Helga, Olenka. Short forms: Oli, Ollie, Olly.

**Olive**: See Olivia.

**Olivia**: From the Latin *oliva* meaning 'olive'. Alternative spellings: Oliva, Olive, Olivette. Short forms: Liv, Livia, Livvy, Livy, Oli, Ollie, Olly.

**Olwen**: From the Welsh meaning 'white footprint'. Alternative spellings: Olwyn.

**Olympia**: From the Greek meaning 'from Olympus'. Alternative spellings: Olympe, Olimpia, Olympie.

**Ondine**: See Undine.

**Ondrea**: See Andrea.

**Onora**: See Honora.

**Oonagh**: From the Irish Gaelic meaning 'lamb'. Alternative spellings: Una, Oona.

**Opal**: From the Sanskrit meaning 'jewel' or 'gemstone'.

**Ophelia**: From the Greek meaning 'to help'.

**Ophrah**: From the Hebrew meaning 'young deer' or 'place of dust'. Alternative spellings: Ofra, Ofrah., Ophra, Oprah.

**Ora**: From the Hebrew meaning 'light'.

**Oralia**: The English form of Aurelia. Alternative spelling: Oralie.

**Oriana**: From the Latin meaning 'rising sun' or 'morning sun'.

Alternative spellings: Oria, Oriande, Oriane, Orianne, Oriente.

**Oriel**: From the Latin meaning 'gold'.

**Oriola**: From the Latin meaning 'golden bird'.

**Orla**: From the Gaelic Irish meaning 'golden lady'.

**Osma**: From the Old English meaning 'divine protection'.

**Otilie**: From the Czech meaning 'lucky heroine'.

**Oz**: From the Hebrew meaning 'strength'.

## P

**Padma**: From the Hindi meaning 'lotus'.

**Pagan**: From the Old English meaning 'country dweller'.

**Paige**: From the French meaning 'young attendant' or the Old English meaning 'child'. Alternative spellings: Padge, Padget, Page.

**Paisley**: From the Scottish place name.

**Pallas**: From the Greek meaning 'goddess'.

**Paloma**: From the Spanish meaning 'dove'. Alternative spellings: Palloma, Palomita, Peloma.

**Pamela**: From the Greek meaning 'honey'. Alternative spellings: Pamala, Pammela. Short form: Pam, Pammie, Pammy.

**Pandora**: From the Greek meaning 'highly gifted'.

**Pansy**: From the Greek meaning 'flower' or 'fragrant' or the French *penser* meaning 'to think'.

**Panthea**: From the Greek meaning 'all the gods'.

**Paquita**: See Frances.

**Paris**: See Boys' Names. Alternative spelling: Parris.

**Parvati**: From the Sanskrit meaning 'of the mountain'.

**Pascale**: From the French meaning 'Easter' or the Hebrew *pesach* meaning pass over, relating to the festival of Passover. Alternative spellings: Paschal, Pasquale.

**Pat**: See Patricia or Patience.

**Patience**: From the Latin meaning 'to suffer'. Short forms: Pat, Pattie, Patty.

**Patrice**: See Patricia.

**Patricia**: From the Greek meaning 'noble'. Alternative spellings: Patreece, Patrica, Patrice, Patricka, Patrisha, Patrishia. Short forms: Pat, Patsy, Pattie, Patty, Tricia, Trisha.

**Paula**: A feminine form of Paul (see Boys' Names). Alternative spellings: Paola, Paulene, Pauletta, Paulette, Pauli, Paulie, Paulina, Pauline, Paullette, Pauly, Pol, Polly.

**Paulette**: See Paula.

**Pauline**: See Paula.

**Payton**: A feminine form of Patrick (see Boys' Names). Alternative spelling: Peyton.

**Pearl**: From the Latin meaning 'jewel'.

**Pegeen**: See Margaret. Alternative spelling: Peggeen.

**Peggy**: See Margaret.

**Pelagia**: From the Greek meaning 'mermaid' or 'sea'.

**Penelope:** From the Greek meaning 'weaver'. Short form: Penny.

**Peninah:** From the Hebrew meaning 'coral' or 'pearl'. Short forms: Penina, Peninna.

**Penny:** See Penelope.

**Peony:** From the Greek meaning 'praise-giving' or possibly from the flower.

**Perdita:** From the Latin meaning 'lost'. Short forms: Perdie, Perdy.

**Peri:** From the Greek meaning 'mountain dweller' or the Persian meaning 'fairy' or 'elf'.

**Perri:** From the Greek or Latin meaning 'small rock' or 'traveller'; the French meaning 'pear tree' or the Welsh meaning 'daughter of Harry'. Alternative spellings: Perrie, Perry.

**Persephone:** From the Greek meaning 'dazzling brilliance' or 'she who destroys the light'.

**Peta:** See Petra.

**Petra:** A feminine form of Peter (see Boys' Names). Alternative spellings: Peta, Petrea, Petrina, Pietra.

**Petronella:** From the Greek meaning 'small rock'. Alternative spellings: Patronilla, Pernella, Petrona, Petroneia, Petronelle.

**Petula:** From the Latin meaning 'seeker' or possibly from the Latin meaning 'to ask'. Alternative spelling: Petulah.

**Phedra:** From the Greek meaning 'shining'.

**Pheodora:** See Feodora.

**Philidelphia:** From the Greek meaning 'brotherly love'.

**Phillippa**: The feminine form of Philip (see Boys' Names). Alternative spellings: Philipa, Phillipina, Phillippe, Phillippine. Short forms: Phil, Phillie, Philly, Pippa, Pippy.

**Philomena:** Feminine form of the Latin name *Philomenus* from the Greek *philein* meaning 'to love' and *menos* meaning 'strength'. Alternative spellings: Filomena, Philomene, Philomina. Short forms: Mena.

**Phoebe**: From the Greek meaning 'pure' or 'bright'. Alternative spelling: Phebe.

**Phylicia:** See Felicia. Alternative spellings: Philica, Philycia, Phylesia, Phylisha, Phyllecia.

**Phyllis**: From the Greek meaning 'foliage'. Alternative spellings: Phillis, Philys, Phylis, Phyllys.

**Pia**: From the Italian meaning 'devout'.

**Piedad**: From the Spanish meaning 'devoted' or 'pious'.

**Pilar**: From the Latin meaning 'pillar' or 'column' or possibly from the Spanish *Nuestra Senora del Pilar* meaning 'Our Lady of the Pillar' a name for the Virgin Mary.

**Piper**: From the English meaning 'pipe player'.

**Pippa**: See Phillippa.

**Pippi**: From the French meaning 'rosy-cheeked'.

**Placida**: From the Latin meaning 'serene'.

**Polly**: See Paula or Mary.

**Pomona**: From the Latin meaning 'apple' or 'fruit'.

**Poppy**: From the Latin meaning 'poppy flower'.

**Porshe**: See Portia.

**Portia**: From the Latin meaning 'offering' or possibly from Latin *porcus* meaning 'pig'. Alternative spellings: Porche, Porsha, Porshe, Portiea.

**Posey**: See Josephine.

**Precious**: From the French meaning 'precious' or 'dear'.

**Primrose**: From the Latin meaning 'first rose' or from the flower.

**Priscilla**: From the Latin meaning 'primitive' or 'ancient'. Alternative spellings: Precilla, Pricilla, Priscella, Prisila, Prissilla. Short forms: Cilla, Piri, Pris, Prisca, Prissy.

**Prudence**: From the Latin meaning 'cautious' or 'discreet'. Alternative spellings: Pru, Prudy, Prue.

**Prunella**: From the Latin meaning 'little plum'. Short forms: Pru, Prue.

**Psyche**: From the Greek meaning 'soul'.

## Q

**Queenie**: From the Old English meaning 'Queen'. Alternative spelling: Queeny.

**Quinn**: Possibly from the Old English word *cwen* meaning 'Queen' or the Irish Gaelic *Caoin* meaning 'counsel'.

**Quinta**: From the Latin meaning 'fifth'.

## R

**Raah:** From the Greek meaning 'shepherd' or 'Saviour'.

**Rabiah:** From the Arabic meaning 'fourth' or 'fragrant breeze'. Alternative spellings: Rabia.

**Rachael:** From the Hebrew meaning 'ewe', symbolising innocence. Alternative spellings: Rachel, Rachelle, Raquel, Raquelle. Short forms: Rach, Rae, Ray.

**Rachel:** See Rachael.

**Rachelle:** See Rachael.

**Radha:** From the Sanskrit meaning 'success'.

**Rae:** See Rachael.

**Rafaela:** A feminine form of Raphael (see Boys' Names).

**Rainbow:** From the Old English words *regn* meaning 'rain' and *boga* meaning 'bow' or 'arch'.

**Raine:** From the German meaning 'mighty army' or the French word *reine* meaning 'Queen'. Alternative spelling: Rayne.

**Raisa:** From the Russian meaning 'paradise' or the Yiddish meaning 'rose'. Alternative spelling: Raissa.

**Ramona:** A feminine version of Ramon (see Boys' Names).

**Ranelle:** A feminine form of Rudolf or Randall (See Boys' Names).

**Rani:** From the Hindi meaning 'princess' or 'queen'.

**Raquel:** See Rachel.

**Rasa:** From the Lithuanian meaning 'dew'.

**Raven:** From the English meaning 'blackbird' or the French meaning 'voracious'. Alternative spelling: Ravenne.

**Ravenne:** See Raven.

**Ravette:** From the Old English meaning 'sacred daughter'.

**Rayna:** The feminine form of Raynor (see Boys' Names).

**Reanna:** See Rhiannon.

**Reba:** See Rebecca.

**Rebecca:** From the Hebrew meaning 'tied' implying 'a faithful wife'. Alternative spellings: Rebeca, Rebeka, Rebekah, Rivka, Rivkah. Short forms: Reba, Becca, Reckie, Beka, Bekki, Bex, Riva.

**Reece:** See Boys' Names. Alternative spellings: Reace, Reese, Riece, Rice.

**Regan:** Possibly the Irish *riogan* meaning 'queen' or from the Gaelic surname O Riagáin. Alternative spelling: Reagan, Reagen.

**Regina:** From the Latin meaning 'queen'. Alternative spellings: Reena, Reene, Regan, Reggie, Regine, Reina, Rena, Rene, Rina. Short forms: Gina, Geena.

**Reiko:** From the Japanese meaning 'gratitude'.

**Reine:** From the Latin meaning 'queen'. Alternative spelling: Reina.

**Renata:** From the Hebrew meaning 'joy' or 'song' or the Latin meaning 'born again'.

**René:** From the French meaning 'reborn'. Alternative spellings: Renee, Reenie.

**Renée:** From the Latin *Renata* meaning 'reborn'.

**Rexanne**: See Roxanne.

**Rhea**: From the Greek meaning 'flowing stream' or 'protectress'.

**Rhian**: See Rhiannon.

**Rhiannon**: From the Welsh meaning 'goddess' or 'maiden'. Alternative spellings: Reanna, Reanne, Rheanna, Rhian, Rhianna.

**Rhoda**: From the Greek meaning 'rose' or possibly 'woman of Rhodes'.

**Rhona**: From the Scottish meaning 'rough isle' or 'fierce waters'.

**Rhonda**: From the Welsh *rhon* meaning 'lance' or 'pike' and *da* meaning 'good' or the Celtic meaning 'powerful river'.

**Rhonwen**: From the Welsh meaning 'fair'.

**Ria**: See Maria.

**Ricarda**: A feminine form of Richard (see Boys' Names). Alternative spelling: Richarda. Short forms: Ricky, Rikki.

**Richelle**: A feminine form of Richard (see Boys' Names) or from the Old English *ric* meaning 'power'.

**Ricky**: See Ricarda. Alternative spelling: Rikki.

**Riley**: From the Gaelic Irish meaning 'valiant'.

**Rilla**: From the Spanish meaning 'little stream' or 'little brook'.

**Rina**: A short form of Carina, Katerina or Rionach or from the Hebrew meaning 'joyful'.

**Riona**: From the Irish Gaelic name *rioghan* meaning 'queen'.

**Rionach**: From the Gaelic Irish meaning 'queenly'.

**Risa:** From the Latin meaning 'laughter'.

**Rita:** See Margaret.

**Riva:** See Rebecca.

**Roberta:** The feminine form of Robert (see Boys' Names). Short forms: Bobbette, Bobbi, Bobbie, Bobby, Bobbye, Bobina, Bobinette, Rebinah, Robbie, Robena, Robenia, Robin, Robina, Robine, Robinette, Robinia, Robyn, Rori, Rory, Ruby.

**Robin:** See Roberta.

**Rochelle:** From the Old German *hrok* meaning 'rest' or the French meaning 'little rock'; see also Rachelle.

**Roderica:** From the German meaning 'famous ruler'. Short forms: Rori, Rory.

**Róisín:** From the Irish meaning 'rose'.

**Rolanda:** The feminine form of Roland (see Boys' Names).

**Romy:** A short form of Rosemary.

**Ronalda:** The feminine form of Ronald (see Boys' Names). Short forms: Rona, Roni, Ronna, Ronne, Ronnie.

**Roni:** From the Hebrew meaning 'song'; see also Ronaldo.

**Ronnie:** See Ronaldo or Veronica.

**Rosa:** From the Latin meaning 'rose'; see also Rosamond or Rosalind. Alternative spellings: Rosalie.

**Rosabel:** From the Latin words *rosa* meaning 'rose' and *belle* meaning 'beautiful'. Alternative spellings: Rosabella, Rosabelle.

**Rosaleen:** See Rosalind.

**Rosalind**: From the Old German *hros* meaning 'horse' and *lind* meaning 'weak', 'tender' or 'soft'. Alternative spellings: Rosaleen, Rosaline, Rosalyn, Rosalynn, Rosalynne, Roslyn. Short forms: Ros, Rosa, Rose, Roz.

**Rosamond**: From the Latin meaning 'rose of the world' or 'rose of purity' or the German meaning 'protector of the horse'. Alternative spellings: Rosamunde. Short forms: Ros, Rosa, Rose, Roz.

**Rose**: From the Old German meaning 'fame' or the flower; see also Rosalind, Rosamond. Alternative spellings: Rosie, Rosey.

**Roseanne**: The combination of Rose and Anne.

**Rosemary**: From the Latin *ros marinus* meaning 'sea dew'. Alternative spelling: Rosemarie. Short form: Roma.

**Rosetta**: From the Latin meaning 'little rose'.

**Roshan**: From the Sanskrit meaning 'shining light'.

**Rowan**: From the Irish Gaelic meaning 'little red one'; possibly the Celtic meaning 'clad in white' or from the tree. Alternative spelling: Rowen.

**Rowena**: From the Celtic meaning 'white skirt'; the Welsh meaning 'fair one' or the German *hrod* meaning 'fame' and *wynn* meaning 'joy'.

**Roxanne**: From the Persian meaning 'dawn'. Alternative spellings: Rexanne, Rosana, Roxana, Roxane, Roxanna, Roxie, Roxine, Roxy.

**Roya:** The feminine form of Roy (see Boys' Names).

**Ruby:** From the Latin word *rubinus* meaning 'red'.

**Rumer:** From the English gypsies possibly derived from 'Romany'.

**Runa:** From the Norse meaning 'to flow'.

**Ruta:** From the Lithuanian meaning 'rue' (the herb).

**Ruth:** From the Hebrew meaning 'vision of beauty' or 'companion'. Short forms: Ruthi, Ruthie.

**Ryan:** See Boys' Names. Alternative spellings: Rian, Rion, Ryana, Ryann, Ryen.

**Ryesen:** From the English meaning 'rye' or the Irish Gaelic name *Roisin* meaning 'rose'.

## S

**Saada:** From the Hebrew meaning 'support' or 'help'. Alternative spelling: Sada.

**Saba:** From the Hebrew meaning 'old'.

**Sabah:** From the Arabic meaning 'morning dawn'.

**Sabelle:** See Isabelle.

**Sabina:** See Sabine.

**Sabine:** From the Latin meaning 'of the Sabines' an ancient people living in central Italy. Alternative spellings: Sabina, Savina.

**Sable:** From the Slavic meaning 'black'.

**Sabra:** From the Hebrew or Arabic meaning 'thorny'.

**Sabrina:** From the Latin meaning 'the boundary mark' or the

Hebrew meaning 'thorny'. Alternative spellings: Sabreena, Sabrena, Sabryna, Zabrina.

**Sacha**: From the Greek meaning 'help mate'; see also Alexandra. Alternative spelling: Sasha.

**Sada**: From the Old English *saed* meaning 'seed' or the Hebrew meaning 'support' or 'help'; see also Saada or Sarah. Alternative spellings: Sadele, Sadelle, Sadie, Sady.

**Sade**: From the Yoruban African meaning 'honour confers a crown'.

**Sadie**: See Sarah.

**Saffron**: From the Arabic meaning 'crocus'. Short forms: Saffie, Saffy.

**Sage**: From the English meaning 'wise one'.

**Sahara**: From the Arabic meaning 'desert'.

**Salena**: See Selina or Celine.

**Sal**: See Sarah.

**Salima**: From the Arabic meaning 'unharmed'.

**Sally**: See Sarah.

**Salome**: From the Aramaic meaning 'peace'. Alternative spellings: Saloma, Salomi.

**Sam**: See Samantha or Samara.

**Samantha**: From the Aramaic meaning 'listener'. Short forms: Sam, Sami, Sammie, Sammy.

**Samara**: From the Hebrew meaning 'guarded by God'. Short

forms: Sam, Sami, Sammie, Sammy.

**Samira**: From the Arabic meaning 'to talk in the evening or night' or Arabic meaning 'pleasant' or 'entertainer'. Short forms Sam, Sami, Sammi, Sammy.

**Sancha**: From the Latin meaning 'holy' or 'pure'. Alternative spellings: Cynthia, Sanchia.

**Sandra**: See Alexandra. Alternative spellings: Sandrea, Saundra, Sondra, Zandra. Short forms: Sandee, Sandi, Sandy.

**Sandrine**: From the French version from Alexandra.

**Santa**: From the Latin *sanctus* meaning 'holy'. Alternative spellings: Santana, Santina.

**Saoirse**: From the Irish Gaelic meaning 'freedom'.

**Sapphire**: From the Arabic meaning 'beautiful' or the Sanskrit meaning 'beloved of Saturn'. Alternative spellings: Safira, Sapphira.

**Sara**: See Sarah.

**Sarah**: From the Hebrew meaning 'princess'. Alternative spellings: Morag, Sada, Sadella, Sadie, Saira, Sairah, Sara, Sari, Sarina, Sarri, Sal, Sally, Shara, Shari, Sherrie, Sorcha, Zara, Zarah, Zaria, Zoreen, Zorna.

**Saraid**: From the Celtic meaning 'excellent'.

**Sasha**: See Sacha.

**Saskia**: Possibly from the word *sachs* meaning 'Saxon'.

**Saturnia**: From the Latin *satus* meaning 'sowing' or 'planting'.

**Savannah**: From the Spanish *zavana* meaning 'an expanse of open grassland'. Alternative spelling: Savanna, Savonne.

**Scarlet**: From the Old French referring to the colour. Alternative spelling: Scarlett.

**Sebastiane**: The feminine form of Sebastian (see Boys' Names). Alternative spellings: Sebastene, Sebastia, Sebastiana, Sebastienne.

**Sela**: From the Hebrew meaning 'rock'.

**Selima**: From the Arabic meaning 'peaceful'.

**Selina**: From the Greek meaning 'moon goddess'. Alternative spellings: Celina, Salena, Selena, Selenia, Selene, Selenna, Selinda, Seline. Short form: Sena.

**Selma**: From the Celtic meaning 'fair' or the Norse meaning 'divinely protected'.

**Sena**: See Selina.

**Senga**: From the Scottish Gaelic *eang* meaning 'slender'.

**Seonaid**: See Janet.

**September**: From the Latin *septum* meaning 'seven'.

**Septima**: From the Latin meaning 'seventh'.

**Serafina**: From the Hebrew word *seraphim* meaning 'burning ones'. Alternative spellings: Sarafina, Serafine, Seraphina, Seraphine, Serapia, Serofina.

**Seren**: From the Welsh meaning 'star'.

**Serena**: From the Latin *serenus* meaning 'calm' or 'serene'.

Alternative spellings: Sirena, Sirenna, Syrena.

**Serenity**: From the Latin *serenus* meaning 'calm' and 'serene'.

**Sevina**: From the Latin *sevérus* meaning 'severe' or 'stern'.

**Shaina**: From the Hebrew meaning 'beautiful'; see also Shana. Alternative spelling: Shayna.

**Shakira**: From the Arabic meaning 'thankful'. Alternative spelling: Shaira.

**Shalaidah**: From the Old Celtic meaning 'wood nymph' or 'from the fairy wood'.

**Shaley**: From the Old English *shelley* meaning 'clearing on/near a slope'.

**Shana**: From the Irish meaning 'old' or 'wise'. Alternative spellings: Danna, Shan, Shanda, Shandi, Shane, Shannah.

**Shania**: Possibly an English name derived from Shana or from the Native American meaning 'on my way'.

**Shannagh**: Possibly from the Irish Gaelic meaning 'old' or 'wise'.

**Shannon**: From the Irish Gaelic meaning 'wise' or from the name of an Irish river.

**Sharayah**: From the Hebrew meaning 'friend'.

**Sharlene**: See Charlene.

**Sharmilla**: From the Sanskrit meaning 'happy'.

**Sharon**: From the Hebrew meaning 'plain' or 'flat area'. Alternative spellings: Shareen, Sharron, Sharyn.

**Shawna**: The feminine form of Shawn (see Boys' Names).

**Shauna**: See Shona.

**Shayla**: See Sheila.

**Shayna**: From the Hebrew meaning 'beautiful' or 'fine' or 'goodly'.

**Shayne**: The feminine form of Shane (see Boys' Names).

**Shea**: From the Irish meaning 'courteous'.

**Sheba**: See Bathsheba.

**Sheena**: A Gaelic form of Jane.

**Sheila**: From the Irish Gaelic *sile* meaning 'blind'; see also Celene. Alternative spellings: Shayla, Sheelagh, Sheelah, Shelagh, Shelia, Shelli, Shelly, Shielah.

**Shelby**: From the English meaning 'willow farm'; see also Shelly.

**Shelda**: See Sheldon.

**Sheldon**: Originally an English surname taken from the local areas in Derbyshire and Devon. Short form: Shelda.

**Shelley**: From the English meaning 'meadow on the ledge'; see also Michelle. Alternative spelling: Shelli, Shelby.

**Sheree**: From the French *chérie* meaning 'dear' or 'darling'. Alternative spellings: Shereen, Sheri, Sherri, Sherrie, Sherry.

**Shereen**: See Sheree.

**Sheridan**: From the Gaelic Irish meaning 'bright' or possibly 'to seek'.

**Sherilyn**: A blend of Sheryl and Marilyn.

**Sherry**: See Sheree.

**Sheryl**: See Cheryl.

**Shirley**: From the Old English *scir* meaning 'shire' and *leah* meaning 'meadow'. Alternative spellings: Sheree, Sherill, Sherl, Sherri, Sherrie, Sherye, Sheryl, Shirl, Shirlee, Shirleen, Shirlene.

**Shyla**: From the Hindi meaning 'daughter of the mountain'.

**Shona**: A feminine form of Sean (see Boys' Names). Alternative spellings: Shaina, Shaine, Shana, Shanie, Shannon, Shayna, Shayne, Shonda, Shoni, Shonie.

**Shoshana**: From the Hebrew meaning 'lily'. Alternative spellings: Shoshan, Shushan, Shushanah, Shoshanah, Siùsaidh, Sosanna, Sukey, Suki, Sukie, Susan, Susanna, Susanne, Suzanna, Suzanne, Suzette, Zsuzsana, Zuzana,. Short forms: Su, Susan, Sue, Sukey, Susie, Susy, Suzey, Suzie, Suzy.

**Shula**: See Shulamit.

**Shulamit**: From the Hebrew meaning 'peacefulness'. Short form: Shula.

**Shyama**: From the Sanskrit meaning 'dark'.

**Sian**: See Jane. Alternative spelling: Siana.

**Sibyl**: See Cybil. Alternative spellings: Sibil, Sibilla, Sibille, Sibley, Sibylla, Sibyllina, Sybella, Sybil, Sybille, Sybyl, Sybylla.

**Sidney**: See Boys' Names. Alternative spellings: Cydney, Sidoney, Sidonie, Sidonia, Sydney. Short form: Sid, Syd.

**Sidra**: From the Arabic meaning 'star-like'.

**Sidonie**: See Sidney. Alternative spelling: Sidonia.

**Sidra**: From the Latin meaning 'star'.

**Sienna:** From the Italian city.

**Sierra:** From the Spanish meaning 'beautiful mountains'.

**Signa:** From the Latin meaning 'signal'.

**Siegfrieda:** The feminine form of Siegfried (see Boys' Names).

**Sigrid:** From the Scandinavian meaning 'beautiful' or 'victorious'; see also Siegfrieda. Short form: Siri.

**Sigmunda:** The feminine form of Sigmund (see Boys' Names).

**Silvana:** See Silvia.

**Silvia:** From the Latin *silva* meaning 'wood'. Alternative spellings: Silvana, Silvano, Silvannam, Silvina, Sylverta, Sylvi, Sylvia, Sylvie, Sylvina, Sylvonna, Zilvia.

**Simone:** From the French meaning 'hear' or 'listen' or the feminine form of Simon (see Boys' Names). Alternative spellings: Simona, Simonne, Symone.

**Sineád:** A Gaelic Irish form of Jane.

**Siobhán:** A Gaelic form of Jane.

**Sirena:** From the Greek *seiren* meaning 'to bind' or 'to attack'; see also Serena.

**Siri:** From the Scandinavian goddess of humour; see also Sigrid.

**Sirios:** From the Greek meaning 'glowing' or 'burning'.

**Sisley:** See Cecilia.

**Skye:** From the Scottish Island; see also Skyla.

**Skyla:** From the Dutch meaning 'scholar' or possibly 'sheltering'. Alternative spellings: Skyler. Short forms: Sky, Skye.

**Slaney:** From the Irish Gaelic meaning 'challenge'.

**Sloane:** From the Scottish Gaelic meaning 'fighter' or 'warrior'. Alternative spelling: Sloan.

**Sofia:** See Sophia. Alternative spellings: Sofiah, Sofie, Sophie.

**Soma:** From the Sanskrit meaning 'moon' or the Greek meaning 'body'.

**Sona:** From the Latin meaning 'to make a noise' or 'to cry out'.

**Sonaya:** See Sonya.

**Sonya:** From the Greek *sofya* meaning 'wisdom'. Alternative spellings: Sonia, Sonja, Sonya, Sofia, Sofie, Sophia, Sophie.

**Sophia:** See Sonya.

**Sophie:** See Sonya.

**Soraya:** From the Persian meaning 'princess'.

**Sorcha:** From the Gaelic meaning 'bright'; see also Sarah.

**Sorrel:** From the planet of the same name or the Old French meaning 'sour'.

**Sri:** From the Sanskrit meaning 'light' or 'beauty'.

**Stacey:** Possibly from Anastasia or the Greek meaning 'rich in corn'; also the feminine form of Eustace (see Boys' Names). Alternative spellings: Stace, Staci, Stacie, Stacy, Statsia.

**Star:** From the Latin *stella* meaning 'star'.

**Stella:** From the Latin meaning 'star'; see also Estella.

**Stephanie:** The feminine form of Stephen (see Boys' Names). Alternative spellings: Stefana, Stefani, Stefania, Stefanie,

Steffanie, Steffany, Steffi, Stephani, Stephania, Stephany, Stephine, Stevie.

**Sudy**: From the Old English meaning 'south' or 'southerly wind'.

**Suki**: From the Japanese meaning 'beloved'.

**Summer**: From the Old English *sumor* meaning 'summer'. Alternative spelling: Somer.

**Sunita**: From the Sanskrit meaning 'well-behaved'.

**Sunni**: See Sunny or the Scandinavian name Sunniva meaning 'gift of the sun'.

**Sunny**: From the Old English *sunne* meaning 'bright' or 'sunny' or 'cheerful'. Alternative spelling: Sunni.

**Susan**: See Shoshana.. Short form: Sukey.

**Susanna**: See Shoshana.

**Suzanne**: See Shoshana.

**Suzette**: See Shoshana.

**Svetlana**: From the Russian meaning 'bright light'.

**Sybil**: See Cybil.

**Sydney**: See Boys' Names.

**Sylvestra**: The feminine form of Silvester (see Boys' Names).

**Sylvia**: See Silvia.

## T

**Tabitha**: From the Aramaic meaning 'gazelle'. Alternative spelling: Tabatha. Short forms: Tab, Tabbie, Tabby.

**Talitha**: From the Aramaic meaning 'little girl'. Alternative spelling: Talia.

**Tallulah:** From the Gaelic meaning 'abundance' or 'lady' or the Native American meaning 'bubbling spring'.

**Talya**: See Natalya.

**Tamar**: From the Arabic *tamr* meaning 'date farm' or the Hebrew meaning 'palm tree'. Short forms: Tam, Tami, Tammie, Tammy, Tamy.

**Tamara**: From the Arabic meaning ' palm tree' or 'seed of the palm tree'. Short forms: Tam, Tami, Tammie, Tammy, Tamy.

**Tamarind**: From the Arabic *tamr hindi* meaning 'Indian date palm'. Short forms: Tam, Tami, Tammie, Tammy, Tamy.

**Tamsin**: A feminine form of Thomas (see Boys' Names). Alternative spellings: Tamsyn, Tamzen, Tamzin. Short forms: Tam, Tami, Tammie, Tammy, Tamy.

**Tania**: From the Russian meaning 'fairy queen'; see also Tatiana. Alternative spelling: Tanya.

**Tanith**: From the Phoenician goddess of love or the Old Irish *tan* meaning 'estate'. Alternative spellings: Tanit, Tanis.

**Tara**: From the Irish Gaelic meaning 'hill'.

**Tarina**: From the Hebrew meaning 'legend' or 'story'.

**Tasha**: From the Russian meaning 'independent'; see also Natasha.

**Tasnim**: From the Arabic meaning 'paradise fountain'.

**Tate**: From the Scandinavian meaning 'cheerful'.

**Tatiana**: From the Russian after the King Tatius of the Sabines. Short form: Tania.

**Tatum**: From the Middle English *tayt* meaning 'cheerful', 'spirited'.

**Tavia**: See Octavia.

**Tawny**: From the Irish meaning 'a green field'.

**Taya**: Possibly from the Italian or Latin meaning 'unknown'. Alternative spelling: Tèa.

**Tegan**: From the Old Cornish meaning 'ornament'; the Welsh *tegwen* meaning 'fair' or 'pretty'; the Gaelic *tadhg* meaning 'philosopher' or the Celtic meaning 'doe'. Alternative spelling: Teagen.

**Tegwen**: From the Welsh meaning 'beautiful', 'fair' or 'pretty'.

**Teresa**: From the Greek meaning 'harvest'. Alternative spellings: Theresa, Thérèsa. Short form: Tess, Tessa, Terri.

**Tess**: See Teresa.

**Tessa**: See Teresa.

**Thalia**: From the Greek *thallein* meaning 'to flourish'.

**Thea**: See Dorothea.

**Thelma**: From the Greek meaning 'wish' or 'will'.

**Theodora**: From the Greek meaning 'gift of God'.

**Thomasina**: A feminine form of Thomas (see Boys' Names).

**Thora**: From the Norse meaning 'the thunderer'.

**Tia**: A short form of Cynthia or Letitia.

**Tiffany**: From the Greek meaning 'manifestation of God'.

**Tina**: See Christina.

**Toni**: See Antonia.

**Topaz**: Named after the gemstone.

**Tracy**: From the *tractare* Latin meaning 'to manage', 'handle', 'lead', 'follow' or 'investigate'. Alternative spellings: Traci, Tracey. Short forms: Trace.

**Tricia**: See Patricia. Alternative spelling: Trisha.

**Trina**: See Katrina.

**Trixie**: See Beatrix.

**Trudy**: From the German meaning 'strength'.

## U

**Ula**: From the Old English meaning 'owl'; the Irish meaning 'sea jewel' or the Old German meaning 'inheritor'.

**Ulla**: From the German or Swedish meaning 'wilful'; see also Ursula.

**Ulrica**: From the German meaning 'wolf ruler' or 'ruler of all'. Alternative spellings: Ulrika, Ulrike, Ullrica, Ullrika. Short forms: Uli, Ully.

**Uma**: From the Hindi meaning 'mother'.

**Una**: See Oonagh.

**Undine**: From the Latin meaning 'wave'. Alternative spellings: Ondine, Undina.

**Unity**: From the English meaning 'unity'.

**Ursula:** From the Latin meaning 'little she-bear'. Alternative spellings: Ursala, Ursela, Ursella, Ursilla, Ursola. Short forms: Ula, Ursa.

**Uta:** From the German meaning 'rich'.

## V

**Valentia:** From the Latin *valens* meaning 'strong' and 'healthy'. Alternative spellings: Valentin, Valentine.

**Valerie:** From the Latin *valere* meaning 'to be strong' or 'to be healthy'. Alternative spellings: Valetta, Valora.

**Valetta:** See Valerie.

**Vanessa:** Created by the *Gulliver's Travels* author Jonathan Swift for his friend Esther Vanhomrigh by taking the first syllable of her surname and Essa, a pet form of Esther. Alternative spelling: Venessa. Short forms: Ness, Nessa, Nessie.

**Vashti:** From the Persian meaning 'beautiful'.

**Vedrana:** From the Yugoslavian *vedra* meaning 'bright' or 'happy'.

**Venetia:** Possibly from the Latin meaning 'of Venice' or the Latin word *venia* meaning 'kindness', 'mercy', 'forgiveness'.

**Vera:** From the Latin meaning 'true' or the Russian meaning 'faith'.

**Verena:** From the Latin meaning 'truthful'.

**Verity:** From the Latin meaning 'truth' or 'truthful'.

**Veronica:** From the Latin *vera icon* meaning 'true image'. Alternative spellings: Véronic, Veronika, Véronique. Short forms: Roni, Ronnie, Ronny, Veron.

**Victoria**: From the Latin meaning 'victory'. Alternative spellings: Victoire, Viotoriana, Victorie, Vicrtorina, Viktoria, Vitoria, Vittoria. Short form: Vicki, Vickie, Vicks, Vicky, Viki, Vikki, Vix.

**Viola**: From the Latin word *violetta* meaning 'violet'.

**Virginia**: From the Latin *virginitas* meaning 'pure' or possibly from the Latin *virginius* meaning 'manly race'. Short forms: Ginnie, Ginny, Ginger Jinny.

**Vita**: From the Latin meaning 'life'.

**Vivian**: From the Latin meaning 'living', 'alive'. Alternative spelling: Vivien, Vivienne.

## W

**Wanda**: From the Old Norse meaning 'young shoot' or 'a slender stick' or the German meaning 'wanderer'. Alternative spellings: Wende, Vanda.

**Wenda**: From the Gaelic meaning 'fair' or the Old Norse meaning 'to change course', 'to move forward', 'to travel'.

**Wendy**: Created by J M Barrie in *Peter Pan*.

**Whitley**: From the Middle English meaning 'white meadow'.

**Whitney**: From the Middle English meaning 'by the white island'.

**Wilfrida**: The feminine form of Wilfred (see Boys' Names).

**Wilhelmina**: A feminine form of William (see Boys' Names). Alternative spellings: Wilhelma, Willetta, Wilmena. Short forms: Bill, Billie, Billy, Minnie, Willa, Willi, Willy, Wilma.

**Wilma**: See Wilhelmina.

**Winifred**: From the Welsh meaning 'blessed reconciliation' or the Old English meaning 'friend of peace'. Alternative spellings: Winefred, Winfred. Short forms: Fred, Freda, Freddi, Freddie, Fredi, Win, Winnie, Winny, Wyn.

**Winona**: From the Native American Soux meaning 'first-born daughter'. Alternative spelling: Wynona.

**Wynne**: From the Old English word *wine* meaning 'friend'; the Celtic meaning 'fair maiden'; the Welsh meaning 'white', 'light-skinned' or possibly short forms of Blodwyn, Guinivere, Gwyneth.

## X

**Xandra**: See Alexandra.

**Xanthe**: From the Greek meaning 'gold' or 'yellow-haired'. Alternative spelling: Xantha, Zanthe.

**Xena**: From the Greek meaning 'distant place' or 'hospitable'.

**Xenia**: From the Greek meaning 'hospitality'. Alternative spelling: Zenia.

## Y

**Yasmine**: From the Arabic meaning 'jasmine flower'. Alternative spellings: Yasmeen, Yasmin, Yasmina, Yasmine.

**Yelena**: See Helena.

**Yolande**: From the Greek meaning 'violet' or the Latin meaning 'modest'. Alternative spelling: Yolanda.

**Ysabel**: See Isabel.

**Yseult**: See Isolde.

**Yvette**: See Yvonne .

**Yvonne**: From the French meaning 'Yew'. Alternative spellings: Ivette, Yvette.

## Z

**Zabrina**: See Sabrina.

**Zahrah**: From the Arabic meaning 'flower blossom'. Alternative spellings: Zahara, Zaharah, Zahra.

**Zaina**: From the Arabic meaning 'beautiful'.

**Zandra**: See Sandra.

**Zanthe**: See Xanthe.

**Zara**: From the Arabic meaning 'splendour' or from Arabic *zahr* meaning 'flower'; see also Sarah.

**Zarria**: From the Arabic word *zahr* meaning 'flower'.

**Zelda**: Possibly from the Yiddish name *Zelde* meaning 'happiness and good fortune' or a shortened form of Griselda.

**Zenia**: See Xenia.

**Zenobia**: From the Greek *zen* meaning 'gift' and *bios* meaning 'life'. Alternative spellings: Xenobia.

**Zeta**: Uncertain meaning, possibly from the English meaning 'rose'.

**Zhane**: Possibly from the Arabic meaning 'to shine'. Alternative spellings: Shane.

**Zillah**: From the Hebrew meaning 'shade'.

**Zinah**: From the Arabic meaning 'adornment'. Alternative spellings: Zina.

**Zipporah**: From the Hebrew meaning 'bird'. Alternative spellings: Zippora.

**Zita**: From the Italian meaning 'a girl'; the Greek *zetein* meaning 'to seek' or the Spanish meaning 'rose'.

**Zoe**: From the Greek meaning 'life'. Alternative spellings: Zoë, Zola.